HOME
BODYBUILDING

Also by Robert Wolff, Ph.D.

*Bodybuilding 101: Everything You Need to Know
to Get the Body You Want*

Robert Wolff's Book of Great Workouts

HOME
BODYBUILDING

Three Easy Steps
to Building Your Body
and Changing Your Life

By Robert Wolff, Ph.D.

Adams Media Corporation
Avon, Massachusetts

Published by Adams Media Corporation,
57 Littlefield Street, Avon, MA 02322. U.S.A.

ISBN: 1-58062-597-5

Printed in Canada.

J I H G F E D C B A

Library of Congress Cataloging-in-Publication Data
Wolff, Robert, Ph. D.
Home bodybuilding : three easy steps to building your
body and changing your life / by Robert Wolff.
p.   c.m
ISBN 1-58062-597-5
1. Bodybuilding. 2. Home gyms. I. Title.

GV546.5 .W67   2002
646.7'5--dc21   2001055309

Cover and interior photgraphs by Michael Neveux.

This book is available for quantity discounts for bulk purchases.
For information call 1-800-872-5627.

Visit our home page at *www.adamsmedia.com*

Table of Contents

Part IV — Body Specific

Part V — The Mind

PREFACE

Never before has it been so easy to get in shape, eat right, and look and feel your best. So why is it that so many people are getting lazier and fatter? Doesn't make much sense to me.

I mean, come on, most of us know that a little exercise each day helps us look and feel good. Okay, no mystery there. And most of us know what's nutritious and what's not. Don't need a college degree for that one. Most of us know, too, that no pill or miracle infomercial product will give us the body we want. Admit it, it's true.

So what to do? Let's start by doing something—make that *anything*—that will get your blood pumping, your lungs breathing, and your muscles working. Friend, I'm here to tell you it doesn't take much to make a big difference in your life.

And I'm going to let you in on a little secret: The thing that keeps people eating more and doing less isn't lack of knowledge but lack of motivation and belief in themselves. Deep down they

don't believe they deserve to look and feel great. And how can you become and stay motivated to do anything if you don't believe in your ability or worthiness to accomplish it?

I know, the gurus you read and watch tell you that diet or exercise is your problem, but your diet and your failure to exercise are only the *effects* and not the *causes* of all the wrong beliefs you've been telling yourself and have accepted as fact all these years.

You see, when your mind doesn't believe you can have a great-looking and energetic body, it finds ways to keep you right where you are—out of shape and lethargic. It's time we unlocked the chains that have held you for much too long.

In this book, I'm going to tell you how you can look and feel great without going to a gym, buying expensive equipment, hiring a personal trainer, or falling for those late-night come-ons that really are too good to be true.

I've spent many years in the fitness business and have worked with the greatest names in the sport. What I've learned will save you years of frustration, help you get to your heart's desire faster, and make it easier and more fun than I think you may have ever imagined.

But even though I may have just the right tips for you, tips that will work better than anything you've experienced, it won't be worth diddlysquat unless you do your part of the deal. A little something each day, just a little, is all I ask.

People often tell me how frustrated they are from all the exercise regimens, diets, and self-help plans they tried that didn't work. They may have bought all the right foods, joined all the right gyms, and hired all the right trainers, but they were missing some of the essential answers that would've given them the success they wanted.

You will find those answers in this book.

Acknowledgments

Many thanks go out to all who helped put this project together.
Special thanks go to these incredible people:

Michael Neveux for his fabulous photography. You're in a class all by yourself, my friend.

Mike Ryan and Sharon Moore for the great look and fun that both of you brought to this project.

Steven Calabro for always keeping the "Los Angeles Office" open.

To Dawn C. Thompson and everyone at Adams Media.

To you, my reader and friend. You're the reason for this book. Thank you.

INTRODUCTION

Working out at home: for some, it's the only way they'll exercise. Others need a gym. I'll show you ways to get gym-quality results without leaving the house. You don't need expensive equipment. You just need the know-how and the determination to apply what you've learned to create the body you want.

Achieving excellent results is so easy. Train intensely and intelligently, eat nutritiously, get plenty of rest, and let your body do everything else. Looking for diet success? It's very simple: *Do more and eat less.* If you are eating more food than your body needs, you gain weight.

I began my workout adventures at home, and even though I do go to a gym every now and then, I still usually train at home. I have no expensive machines (make that no machines at all), only barbells and dumbbells. After twenty years of training, I'm still getting great results. You can too!

Before you begin, allow yourself to experiment; try the things I tell you and try new things you believe might work or interest you. You are

the boss of your body and 100 percent in charge of giving yourself the look and feel you want.

Don't be afraid to make mistakes. I am constantly learning new things, refining techniques and methods of training, adding and subtracting things as my body and level of fitness evolve along with my personal changes. You are human and your dreams and goals change. Allow your training, nutrition, and body to do the same.

Start off slowly. Don't rush or push yourself too hard too quickly. Allow your body enough

time to "break in" to the great new thing you're wanting it to do. It will respond beautifully by becoming firmer and stronger, with energy and vitality that will surprise you.

You are a work of art, a masterpiece. With your desire and this book, your body will soon be too.

Dispelling the Myths

Let's begin with some of those myths we've heard for so long. Where these myths came from is anybody's guess, but one thing's for sure, people still recite and accept them as fact, and it's high time we changed that. Here are twenty of the best ones I've heard.

Myth #1: "You Need to Exercise a Lot"

Who started this hogwash? Unless you feel the need to always be doing something, then the actual exercise time it takes to give you great results is very little. *It's not a matter of how long you work out, it's what you do when you work out.*

If you do endless set after set and exercise after exercise, but aren't doing the right kind of exercise for your body at the right intensity, then much of your time and effort is wasted.

However, once you start doing the best exercises for you and start making your body work more effectively simply by changing the way you do those exercises, then get ready for some major improvements. In other words, you'll be getting better results in less time. Stay tuned. In a few pages I'll show you how.

Myth #2: "You're Too Old to Change the Way You Look and Feel"

Says who? Scientists and researchers? Not a chance. Their studies show that people from young to old can greatly benefit from exercising. Even those in their nineties can get stronger and build muscle!

This myth was started by people who were either just lazy or frustrated by all the wrong beliefs and information they've followed for all these years.

The truth is, if there is even the slightest spark of a desire inside of you to look and feel a little better, then you will be able to do it. Your desire to change some things in your life already puts you halfway to the finish line. Follow what I'm about to tell you and you'll cross it quickly and with ease.

Myth #3: "You Need Expensive Equipment or a Gym"

Do you own a pair of tennis/athletic shoes? Good. Put them on, go outside, and start walking, and you'll be doing the same thing with the same health benefits as those who walk on expensive treadmills, climb stair step machines, or pedal fancy bikes.

If you've got two arms and two legs, you've got all the equipment you need to exercise your body. I've met people without the full use of all their arms and legs who look and feel great because they used what they had and used it well.

You'll soon see that *it doesn't take high-tech to achieve high-quality results.*

Myth #4: "There's Only One Way to Exercise Correctly"

I know it can be confusing to sort through all the information you've heard. I'm going to help you find what you need for your body, your goals, and your life.

As we talk about changing how you look and feel, stay open to any and everything that you find interesting and might like to try. Don't attach yourself to one set of beliefs and think that one special way of training is better than another, because once you do, you close your mind to all the other possibilities that might also work for you. Let me explain.

Some people believe that you must work out three or more times a week to get the best results. But what if you can only work out two times a week and you're getting great results? Just because you're not able to work out on that third day, does that mean your program is less than a great success? Of course not.

Others believe that you must lift heavy weights to exercise productively and effectively. So does that mean if you use lighter weights or no weights at all, you've only wasted your time on nonproductive exercise? Not if it makes you feel good physically and emotionally.

Still others say that either full-range or short-range movements are the best, and they each have their myriad reasons why. Does that mean if you use one as opposed to the other, you didn't exercise correctly? Of course not.

Use them both. Better yet, *use anything and everything that keeps you excited, interested, motivated, and happy.*

Myth #5: "You Need to Eat All the Time and Buy Expensive Supplements"

Chances are, if you've read that in the magazines, especially the muscle, bodybuilding, and fitness publications, there's a good reason; those magazines stay in business because they sell supplements. Supplement companies advertise all over the pages of them, and many of the magazine publishers and owners sell their own supplements. So it's in their best interests, and not necessarily yours, to promote them.

If you're eating good, nutritious foods, drinking plenty of water, getting plenty of sleep, and exercising regularly, then the only supplement you might wish to take would be a good multivitamin/mineral and perhaps some extra vitamin C and antioxidants. Of course, consult your doctor before using any supplements.

Unless you have some mental need to eat all the time, then don't. A world champion athlete once told me, "I know people say to eat five or six small meals a day, but I just can't do it. I always eat a good breakfast, lunch, and dinner, and if I can add a healthy snack at night, then I do it; if not, no big deal."

We're all different, and when it comes to your nutritional needs, *simply give your body what it needs and not what someone else says it needs.* I'll give you some great guidelines to do it.

Myth #6: "If You've Failed with Many Diets and Exercise Plans Nothing Will Work for You"

Actually, it's great news! You've reached the point where you've found out through trial and error what won't work, and you're closer than ever to finding what will.

Every experience in life can teach you something if you'll only keep your mind open and look for the lesson contained in it.

Think of it like this. You have a goal to look and feel better. There is a final destination, an end point, you wish to reach. So, you buy books, magazines, videos, equipment, and the like, all in hopes they will help you reach your destination.

However, somewhere along the way, something doesn't work, and since you have been trying so many different things at once, you're not really able to tell what works and what doesn't. So, you come to the quick conclusion that all of it doesn't work and you give up, frustrated, yet again.

Let's change all that. After you read this book, you'll know what to try and when, so you will be able to pinpoint what works for you and what doesn't. After all, many times the difference between a million-dollar racehorse and one who doesn't win the big money is only a split second.

In other words, when it comes to changing how you look and feel, it doesn't take much to win big. *Often, the small adjustments are the only things you'll need to give your body exactly what it needs to make big changes quickly.* Stay on track, my friend, and I'll take you to the winner's circle.

Myth #7: "One Machine Is All You Need to Have Great Abs or a Great Body"

The people who keep selling these ab machines on TV are misleading you, friend. It's so easy to be lured into thinking that if only you buy their machine, you'll look like those models. But did you ever notice the fine print disclaimer at the bottom of the TV when the announcer comes on telling you how to order? It says something like this: "Results shown here are not typical" and "blah, blah, blah along with diet and exercise."

Meaning those male and female models with great midsections and bodies who are using those machines didn't get their bodies to look that way simply by using *those* machines.

You can bet your last dollar they spent many years working out at a gym—or at home—and followed a strict diet. But somehow they just didn't have enough time to tell you all that while you were watching them crunch or slide forward and backward.

The truth is, you don't need any machine to look and feel great, so save your money.

Myth #8: "If You Miss Any Workouts, You'll Lose All the Benefit"

It's human nature isn't it? The fear of losing something. Take a good look at your life and see how much this fear influences what you do and don't do. If you're like most people, you're going to be shocked.

Let's start thinking about what you'll gain by exercising and eating right and how much fun it will be and how great it will make you look and feel. And let's put this whole exercise/eating thing in perspective.

Think of exercise as something you did as a kid and you'll do for the rest of your life. See it as a part of your life, just as you would eating and sleeping.

Don't you remember when you were a kid how good it made you feel when you played hard all day and came in at night and slept like a bear in hibernation? Your body was growing, it was lean, you could eat and eat and still not get full, you were healthy and, most of all, you were happy.

Just because you're a few years older—okay, maybe many years older—doesn't mean that has to change. Sure, the kind of exercise you do and the time you have to do it may change, but those great feelings that exercise and being active make you feel can always stay with you.

The results from exercising and eating right are

built over many months and years, and they stay with you. Whenever you miss any workouts or go through days or weeks of not eating your best, don't worry about it. Simply do your best to start back again as soon as you can and you'll be fine.

We live in a society that wants instant results and believes in instant failures. Both these attitudes will only take you down the dead-end road of misery, frustration, and unhappiness. It's time for you to get off it.

Here's something that will help you keep this on-again, off-again thing in its proper perspective. Always remember that all those days, weeks, and months of no exercise and lousy eating will stop the very instant you begin exercising again and eat something nutritious. *The very instant you begin exercising and eating right again is when the old way is over and the new way has begun.* Each day build on it little by little, and you'll be where you want to be very quickly.

Myth #9: "Working Out Makes You Too Tight, Too Stiff, Too Big, or Too Slow"

The people who don't work out are the ones who typically say this, for if they did work out, they'd know just what a crock those statements are.

Working out will help you do every physical thing better than you could if you didn't exercise.

Your body is designed to be worked. Years ago, most of our ancestors made their living from physically working hard.

These days, that's the exception to the rule. So does that mean our bodies have changed and along with it the need to exercise? Not a chance. We need to do it even more now, since so few of us actually do much beyond get up, stand in the shower, get in the car, sit at our desks, and walk from the car to the movie theater, food store, or mall.

I'm not talking about you becoming a world champion athlete—unless of course you want to—but just someone who simply gives his or her body a little exercise regularly.

Don't worry. *What you're about to learn won't make you too big, too small, too thin, too slow, too tight, or too anything else.* It will make you too terrific, but I have a feeling you'll be able to handle that.

Myth #10: "Only Certain People Can Have a Good-Looking and Great-Feeling Body"

Why do people continue to believe this nonsense? And why is it that we keep so many wonderful things—such as a great-looking healthy body—from ourselves? It's almost like we get some sort of perverse reward by neglecting the things that are good for us and denying ourselves the things we want most.

If you're reading this, that means you're alive, and if you're alive, then that's the only prerequisite to looking and feeling great. So relax, you've already passed the test. The rest is easy.

Most people fall into this trap of thinking that unless they can look like the latest model, actor, athlete, or whoever is the latest rage, they will just get depressed and frustrated and lose the desire to look and feel their best.

The truth is that you are the only one who has your body and your look. And if you are smart, you will be proud of that fact and play it to the hilt, just like the celebrities do. That means no one, as much as they might want to or as much as they might try, could ever look like you.

Now, if you're following where I'm going with this, it should start making you smile, because in this world we all want to feel special and unique. *By exercising and eating right and following the tips I'm about to share with you, you will have a good-looking and great-feeling body that can be yours for the rest of your life.* Compare? Don't you dare. The most important person is you!

Myth #11: "You Really Can't Do Much to Change Your Body"

Who told you that? One thing I can guarantee you is that if you don't do anything, you most definitely won't change your body—unless getting more out of shape is what you call a change.

Each of us has our own uniquely shaped body, and even though we're of the same species, we're all a little different. Ultimately, genes are a big factor in how you'll look.

I've met people who were so genetically gifted that their bodies looked like those of elite athletes, yet they did little, if any, training. I've met others who have busted their butts for years, working out and eating right, and still the best they can do is keep the pounds off and maintain a halfway decent shape.

So are you doomed if you have less than a perfect set of genes? Heck no. By doing the right exercises and eating the right kinds of foods for your body, you can sculpt the best body you're capable of achieving and experience the look and feel of being extraordinarily healthy and fit.

There's a lot you can do to change how you look and feel—today—and this book is a good place to start.

Myth #12: "You Need to Eat a Lot of Protein"

Be careful of those "experts" who say that only their way of eating is the best. You'd be surprised to learn that many of these experts (doctors, scientists, researchers, and the like) are actually a bit flabby and out of shape themselves.

Protein is a very important nutrient your body needs each day. So are carbohydrates and fats. Remember that we're talking about balance here. Not too much of one or too little of another nutrient, but a balance of all three.

A lot of people don't get enough protein (the good kind, from lean beef, chicken, turkey, fish, eggs, and nonfat dairy products such as skim milk, yogurt, and cottage cheese) and they wonder why their bodies look and feel like they do. Their nutritious eating is haphazard at best.

The body thrives on regularity. It wants to be fed,

watered, exercised, and rested regularly and performs wonderfully when you do that. The problems come when you don't do that and then start finding miracle cures—such as protein-emphasis diets—that you hope will make up for all the nutritional neglect you've given your body.

Myth #13: "You Need to Eat a Lot of Carbohydrates"

Read myth number 12. I will say that many people eat far too many carbs compared to protein. Whether a carb comes from fruit, vegetables, or grains, ultimately the body breaks it down into a sugar. And the body has a tendency to store too much sugar as excess body fat, especially if you're not burning those sugars at work, being active, or exercising.

By all means, give your body a good balance of carbohydrates from fresh vegetables, some grains, and fruits, but don't overdo it. And pay close attention to how your body reacts to carbohydrates.

If, after you've begun your exercise and eating plan, you find yourself having a hard time losing that last bit of body fat, cut your total number of calories back a bit and make those reductions primarily from carbohydrates and see if that doesn't help. Before embarking on any diet plan, consult your doctor first.

Myth #14: "Finding the Best Workout for Your Body Is Too Difficult"

Human nature is basically lazy. Admit it, don't we want to find the magic exercise, pill, or diet that will "be the one" that will change us for good?

The vast majority of people don't take enough time to find the exercises that work best for their body. So they page through magazines, listen to friends, watch the latest guru on TV, and—presto chango—they're still back where they started.

You're the only one who has your body, your level of experience, your goals and dreams, your genes, and your desire and level of commitment. Only you can know what works best for your body.

Sure, others can suggest things, but free advice is worth about as much as it costs you, and it costs you nothing if you don't try it. By all means, take those things and try them out; see if you can find those things you like and will work.

Once you find what works, remember it, and then find another and another until you've got at least five great exercises for each of your body parts. In this book I'll show you how to create your own workouts for life.

Myth #15: "In the End You'll Fail"

The fear of failure keeps people from living the life they've always dreamed of. It's the same for working out and changing how you look and feel.

Let me tell you something. Every human who has walked this earth has had failures, shortcomings, adversities, and disappointments. These experiences teach us valuable lessons, and life will keep repeating these lessons, albeit in different ways, until we finally get it.

Look at failure as something to look forward to, because failure is feedback. It may be telling you that your plan is a good one but needs to be changed just a little bit in order to work and give you success.

If your exercise or nutrition plan isn't working just the way you want it to, begin by changing only a few things at a time until you find the right combination that works for you.

Anyone who's ever built a great body or achieved success in life has failed and gone on. *Life is filled with women and men whose lives prove that the bigger the failure, the bigger the ultimate success.* You can't have one without experiencing the other.

Myth #16: "The Results Will Stop"

I can tell you that at first the results will come very quickly, because if it's been a while since you got yourself in shape, then your body is very receptive and responsive to any training stimulus.

However, you'll find, like everyone else who works out, that the results do slow down, and that's only normal, so don't sweat it. And look at it like this: when the results start slowing down that means your body is getting stronger, tighter, more in shape.

As you will see, the body responds very quickly to the demands placed upon it. If you give it good workouts, eat right, and get plenty of rest, it's going to respond beautifully. And if you want it to keep responding in that way, then you must constantly vary the stimulus you ask it to do.

Your body habituates—that is, gets used to the same old thing—very fast, and one of the best ways to keep it off guard is to give it something new and different to do each time you work out.

Think about it, if you do the same old barbell curls with the same weight each workout, do you really think your arms will ever get any bigger or stronger? Hardly.

Your arms grew and got stronger months ago when you first starting doing those curls with that particular weight, and unless you change your arm workouts, weight used, and so on, you're only spinning your wheels. Don't think they're going to finally respond to this same workout.

Keep your workouts fresh and new and your body will reward you with results month after month, year after year.

Myth #17: "Working Out Is Too Complicated"

All the "experts" have helped perpetuate this myth. I mean, look at all the books, magazines, TV shows, and infomercials that say their way, their machine, their supplement is the best. With so much information, whom and what do you believe?

The simple way is still the best way. Build your foundation and your workouts with the basic barbell, dumbbell, and bodyweight-only exercises. These are the rocks upon which your body house will stand, and the waves and wind of all the other fads will not crumble it or blow it away.

The only indicator you'll need to know if what you're doing is working or not is the results you get. You might measure those results by how much weight you can lift over a given period of time. Or it may be how you look, or simply a matter of how you feel. If working out makes you feel better and reduces stress, and if you enjoy it and it adds quality to your life, then it's an out-of-the-park home run success.

Pick the way that lets you know if you're getting the results that make you feel good, and when your fitness program needs a few changes, begin at once to make them. Begin by changing only one or two things at a time until you're back to enjoying the success you like.

Myth #18: "You Need to Work Out At Least Three Times a Week to Get Results"

Not so. Does the body actually benefit best from training every other day, three days a week? I've yet to see a conclusive, exhaustive study that states that for all the workouts and intensity levels one can do and use, for all the types of people who train and the experience levels they have, and for all the maximal recuperation it's possible to need (physiologically, neuromuscular, and mental), training three days per week is the absolute best method anyone can use.

Almost all training methods have their plusses and minuses, and the key to your ultimate well-rounded training success will be to incorporate some things from each one that will be ideal for your body, your goals, your experience, and your lifestyle.

If three days a week works for you, then do it. If it doesn't, change it and keep changing it until you find the type of training that really rings your bell. It's out there and easy to find, you just gotta do it.

Myth #19: "Men and Women Must Work Out Differently"

Who started this myth? Besides the obvious common size and strength differences, are they saying that men and women have different arms and legs? Don't they each have two of each and don't those muscles get stronger, tighter, firmer, and bigger by weight training?

Sure, women may tend to stay away from heavy squats and deadlifts for aesthetic reasons, simply because these two exercises tend to thicken the body structure. This doesn't mean, however, that a woman wouldn't get some great results from them.

Much of the dictates of how a man or woman should train come from our inner need to conform our lives and bodies to the whims of what society deems acceptable, sexy, attractive, masculine, feminine, and so on, and has little do with how a woman's or man's body would respond to the same exercises.

Train the way you want; forget what society or anyone thinks or says you should do. Ultimately, you're the only one who walks around inside your skin, and you're the only one who knows what makes you happy.

Myth #20: "Losing Weight Makes You Healthier"

On the surface, this appears to be true. But notice the word *weight*. It should say, "Losing *fat* makes you healthier." Most people equate fitness and nutritional success by simply losing weight. But this isn't necessarily true.

If a person loses too much weight, there's a good chance of also losing valuable lean muscle tissue. Fat is basically inert; it doesn't do much but sit there and take up space. Does that mean all fat is bad? Heavens no! Your body needs a certain amount of fat to keep it healthy, protect your organs, etc. The problem is *excessive* fat.

Lean tissue, on the other hand, is working tissue that needs nutrients to sustain it. That means food, and the more lean tissue one has—within reason, of course—the more calories his or her body will burn.

It may help to think of it like this: lean tissue helps keep your metabolism running, and fat slows it down.

If you're wanting to lose weight, start thinking of losing fat instead of just weight. Set a goal to lose one-half to one pound of fat per week. This is very doable and it's a healthy goal for most women and men.

Remember that a pound of fat has 3,500 calories, and to lose one pound a week, you'll need to either burn 500 extra calories a day, cut out 500 calories a day, or a combination of both—reduce your food consumption by 250 calories a day and increase your activity so that you're burning an extra 250 calories a day, which would be one of the fastest and easiest ways to do it.

I DO NOT KNOW ANYONE WHO HAS
GOT TO THE TOP WITHOUT HARD WORK.
THAT IS THE RECIPE.

—MARGARET THATCHER

WORKING OUT AT HOME: YOUR SECRET WEAPON FOR SUCCESS

What you're about to undertake—working out at home—is one of the best things you can do for your body, heart, and soul. But it can also be one of the toughest, and here's why.

When you go to a gym or have a training partner, you have a different place to go to or someone waiting for you at your scheduled workout, which makes it much harder to blow off. However, the great thing about home training is it's so convenient, and you can do it anytime. That's also the reason why it can become too easy to skip it until tomorrow.

The hardest thing for most people who work out—especially at home—is staying motivated. More people stop working out simply because of lack of motivation, belief, and interest than any other reason. With this book, I'm going to help change that.

In the following pages, you're going to find some good information and tips on nutrition that dispel many of the myths you may have heard for years. You'll find some great exercises that'll

give you wonderful results, too. But you're also going to read something different in a fitness/health book.

Sprinkled throughout the pages of this book are some Life Lessons and Mental Principles I've specially selected from my *Book of Life Lessons*. These lessons and principles will inspire you and teach you how to motivate yourself and use the power of your phenomenal mind to change your beliefs, your body, and your life far faster than anything you may have tried before.

You see, only a very few people know how to use the power of their mind to change their body. In fact, most people do just the opposite; they try to first change their bodies and then hope that change will affect their minds.

Sadly, these are the people who year in, year out, continually go on and off diets and start and stop exercise programs, with little to show for it except years wasted, incredible frustration, and lots of money spent.

So, consider it my gift to you—a little surprise bonus, if you will, for buying this book. Not only are you getting proven exercise and nutrition information that works, but you're also going to be inspired, motivated, and perhaps, for the first time in your life, able to make the power of your mind work for you instead of against you to give you the body and life that you want.

LIFE LESSON

YOU ARE A MIND WITH A BODY
Take care of the inside and the outside will take care of itself.

An old sage once said, "Your body was designed to carry your mind; not the other way around." Here's a little something else for you to ponder: Your body can't think; it only responds to the commands given to it by your mind.

Does your body tell your brain when to breathe? No. Does your body tell your brain when and how to heal a cut? No. Your mind is the command center for anything and everything that happens to your body. Yet most people still believe that fixing the outside first will change the inside.

THE LESSON TO BE LEARNED

Look at the way you look. *You have the body you now have because that's exactly the body you believe you should have.* It fits your picture of the body and performance level you've accepted for yourself to have. It can be no different until you first change the picture in your mind (inside) of how your body should look and feel.

For most people, and hopefully you, that's an uncomfortable thought. Why on earth would you choose to look like this when for so long you've told everyone, and even yourself, that you want to look and feel better? Again, give your mind a new picture to work on and it will show you the ways in which you can achieve it.

Any kind of long-term and lasting change must first come from the inside. See and believe yourself as a smarter, more energetic, healthier, dynamic, enthusiastic, and incredibly blessed and successful person and you will become that person in a very short time. But first you must change the inside, and as you do, the outside will take care of itself.

THE BENEFITS OF HOME TRAINING

You'll find home training will be great for lots of reasons. You will have your own, but here are some common ones.

Train Whenever You Want and for as Long as You Want

Of course, by the time you finish this book, you'll know that you don't need to train very long or very often to get fabulous results.

Let's say you're working out at a gym and you're running late, but your workout isn't finished. Well, that means that you'll have to leave and then come back to the gym and finish it later, which, if you're like most people, is just not going to happen.

When you are working out at home it's so easy to pick up where you left off and you won't have to make time to drive back to the gym and finish.

Convenience

If you have a designated place to train, such as a basement or garage gym, great. However, you can do many of the exercises in this book pretty much anywhere.

Save Huge Amounts of Time for Other Things

By the time you pack up your workout gear, get in the car, fight traffic, get to the gym, get dressed, and actually get out on the gym floor ready to do your first exercise, there's a good chance you'll have wasted about thirty to forty minutes. Add the time you work out, shower, get dressed, get back in the car, fight traffic, and return home, and you can easily have used up over two hours.

Compare that to throwing on some workout clothes and walking a few steps in your house to where you want to exercise. You're looking at about four minutes, and that's if you're a slow dresser.

Comfort

How much more comfortable can you get than working out in the privacy of your home? Forget having to dress in fancy workout clothes like so many people do in gyms or being overly sensitive to how you look or what other people will think of you. Who cares? When you're working out at your own home, you're the only one there, and you can do what you want, the way you want, and not be distracted.

It's Cheaper

With many gym/health club memberships peaking well over $400 a year, working out at home can be much cheaper. For the price of a barbell or dumbbell set you could get the same results as you would at the gym and save hundreds of dollars just in the first year. And if all you want to do is nonweighted, bodyweight-only exercises, you save even more.

Now factor in how much money you will save in gas and, the biggest of all, your valuable time and you've got some powerful reasons to make your home your gym.

It Builds Up Your Confidence and Self-Image

One of the biggest fears that people have is thinking they're too fat, too out of shape, too skinny, or too something else to be seen working out in a gym or health club. This fear keeps so many people from exercising and changing their bodies and lives.

In the beginning, we're all a little afraid of not knowing what to do, of how we look, and of what others think of us. For guys, it tends to be a fear of what other guys will think: "Am I too weak?" "Too skinny?" "Too fat?" "Too out of shape?" "Do I look like a beginner?" "Am I doing the exercise right?" "Do I look confused?"

For women, it tends to be what other women will think: "Are my hips, thighs, butt, legs, abs too fat?" "Am I wearing the right clothes?" "How does my body look in them?" "I don't know anybody here!" and "I feel uncomfortable being here."

Understand that all these fears are natural. With each workout, your confidence will grow. As your body begins to take shape, your confidence will grow as well. As you begin feeling better about yourself, more confidence grows, until you very quickly reach the point where it starts to feel really good being who you are and how you look and feel in your skin.

Home training can be just the confidence builder many people need, since there's no one but you who sees you when you're just beginning. It also helps keep you focused on your workouts and your goals since you don't have all those fears about yourself and other people in the back of your mind that come up at the gym.

Then, as your confidence builds and builds each day, each workout, there's a great chance those fears won't be there if you ever want to go to a gym.

LIFE LESSON

THE BEST WAY TO LEARN ANYTHING IS BY DOING

O Lord, thou givest us everything, at the price of an effort.

—Leonardo da Vinci

In libraries, bookstores, and Internet sites you can find books on virtually any subject you can think of. Whatever it is you want to do, from fitness to anything else, you can find a book on it somewhere.

And while books, magazines, television shows, and seminars can give you a lot of good information about whatever you're interested in, the only way you will ever learn it is by doing it.

The world is filled with people who suffer from analysis paralysis. They study, study, study. They learn facts, figures, and formulas. They write out elaborate game plans. They buy all the equipment and supplies they'll need, yet barely, if at all, get started. Or if they do, it's a half-hearted attempt that always results in half-hearted results.

THE LESSON TO BE LEARNED

If you've never played a musical instrument and someone asks you if you can, don't you dare say no. The truth is, you don't know, because you've never tried. *Always remember that experience has virtually nothing to do with ability.*

You may not have had the experience of playing a musical instrument, painting, speaking, or working out and knowing how to do lots of exercises, but that has nothing to do with your being able to do those things and any others you'd like to do.

The only way you will ever know is if you do it. You've heard the old story of the man who when asked what was the best way to get to Carnegie Hall replied "practice." It was never more true than with working out.

If you don't have all the answers about how to exercise, what to eat, and when or how to finally achieve the body you want, that's okay. You're just like anybody else who started. Myself included. Just know that it's okay to not have all the answers before you start. Just get started, even if you can't do it very well and constantly flub things. Soon, that will all change. Hey, you're only a beginner once, so enjoy it. Things only get better from here.

CHAPTER 3

WHAT YOU CAN EXPECT

I'm not going to promise you anything except that I'm going to give you the information and tips that will change your body if you use them.

As consumers we are used to people promising us the world, then being disappointed by the results. I would like to offer you nothing, but ask that you be open to everything. In this way you will be able to experience results greater than your expectations, stay motivated, and keep looking forward to your next workout.

What You Need to Know

You already have the basic tools you will need to achieve great results for a lifetime. If you've got a body, a good mind, and the desire to take action, then you are halfway there.

What I can give you is the know-how. There are lots of other great books out there to learn from—books on nutrition, books on great workouts, books on different exercises, and so on. I say read as many as you want, because there are nuggets of truth in them all.

But I like to think of this book as the one that will give you a great understanding of mental, physical, motivational, and nutritional ideas that work very well for lots of people. Use as many of the ideas, or as few, as you want.

In life, whether its having a great body or learning a new skill, it helps to ask lots of questions, learn as much as you can from anyone and everyone, and then try out those different things to see what will work for you.

In a very short time, you will learn what is working and what isn't, then you can start creating the right combination of techniques that work and feel best for your body, your goals, and your life.

The Full Circle

It may surprise you that many of the people who have great bodies, ones you admire, actually started their training at home.

And while many of them then joined gyms and health clubs, many of those same people went full circle and returned to working out at home again. They may have done so because of their busy schedules, in order to be able to train whenever they want, or simply for the peace and relaxation of taking time for themselves by themselves. So let it be known that you can have the body and health you want without ever having to leave the house.

It's so easy to look for answers outside of ourselves—as in thinking you must train at a gym or health club or listen to the latest guru or try the latest workout craze. The reality is that you can look and feel great with none or a lot of equipment; it's all up to you.

Buying equipment or going to the gym are only the means to the end, but they are never the goal. These are things you can use to help you get the result that you want (a great body), but they are not necessary for you to achieve it.

In my journeys I've been to places such as China, where the luxury of expensive gyms is unheard of. People there exercise with no equipment at all and don't eat the variety of foods we have in the United States; yet they still achieve spectacular results.

Now you are about to embark on as a journey that can make your body look and feel better. Others may say they know the best way you must travel to get there, but don't listen to them. No one knows what you need except you, and only you can give it to yourself.

Allow yourself the freedom to imagine what you may have never thought possible: looking and feeling great without going to a gym.

It's time for you to go the full circle. From being active as a kid to becoming an active adult, *Home Bodybuilding* is the perfect place to start.

LIFE LESSON

KEEP IT SIMPLE

Nothing is more simple than greatness:
Indeed to be simple is to be great.

—Ralph Waldo Emerson

Why do we try to complicate things in life? Is it a quirk of human nature to say, "If something's easy, it must be wrong"? Since when did struggle equate with significance of accomplishment?

For most people, the more complicated things are—such as workouts, diets, and the like—the more anxiety and stress they feel and the more they feel out of control in their lives. This creates frustration, tension, and unhappiness. You've probably been there. These feelings prevent you from attaining the deep sense of calm that you need to have if you want to operate at your most creative best.

THE LESSON TO BE LEARNED

Life is simple, and yours should be too. In nature, and in your life, simple is more powerful.

Begin at once to look for the simplicity in everything you do. You're going to be amazed at how simple everything in your life can be if only you will start to see it as such. Soon you will learn that simplicity and complexity are only a matter of perception.

You'll also learn that your perceptions, the labels you give things, will determine for you whether something's easy or difficult. *In time you will learn to think of things as easy, and your mind will find ways to prove it so.*

CHAPTER 4

THE KNOW-HOW: QUICK TIPS TO GET AND KEEP YOU GOING

Knowing Form and How to Train

I cannot emphasize strongly enough how important it will be for your long-term fitness success that you train with good form. Training with the proper form will help prevent injuries and allow you to work whatever muscle group you're training better and more effectively.

Over the years, I've seen many people train with terrible form. They must be thinking that by lifting heavy weights they can easily make up with weight what they lack in form. Wrong.

Yes, weight training is built around progressive resistance and the steady progression of lifting heavy weights can give great results. But just lifting heavy weight is far from the only goal when it comes to working out.

You want to have fun, right? Working out shouldn't be some kind of torture you dread doing. You want to "feel" your muscles working as they perform each exercise. This not only helps teach your body how to lift and perform the various exercises, but it also helps you make the very important "mind-to-muscle" connection.

When you begin any exercise, or start using one you haven't done in a while, your body (okay, the neurophysiology of your body) jumps into action by establishing neuron and synapse connections—let's call it a muscle highway—that will help your body become more accustomed to that exercise and perform it more efficiently.

Many people call this action "getting in the groove." And that's not a bad description, because as you're teaching your body new exercises, positions, and form, it's basically establishing a groove, a more direct pathway from brain to muscle, that will help you perform the exercise more efficiently.

Once you find "your groove" (and for all of us it will be slightly different, based on our body structures), then that awkward new exercise becomes easier and more enjoyable to do. It will also help give you better results, since you can now concentrate on making the muscles work harder instead of putting so much thought into just learning how to do the exercise.

Along with the many photographs in this book, you'll also find exercise descriptions that should help you to find your groove.

Environment, Disciplines, and Distractions—How to Make Everything Right for You

If you're going to make a great success of your home workout plan, the first step is to find an environment that doesn't distract you and that actually helps you look forward to training.

It's tough getting excited for your workout when you're dealing with ringing phones, people asking you questions, or the TV or if the location where you have your equipment located is too hot or cold. There are just too many distractions.

Working out should first and foremost be enjoyable, then it should be something that allows you to focus and concentrate on what you're doing so that you can get the best from yourself. You need concentration so you can feel your body doing each exercise and focus completely on how your body is reacting to that exercise. Such focus also helps you pay close attention to exercise form, so you minimize injuries and maximize results.

Music can be a great thing to have playing while you're training, and I highly recommend it. Certain songs have a way of motivating the listener, and if you choose songs that get you going, then it can only help your workout by raising your enthusiasm and intensity.

Many people have told me they've found it best to have their workout area separate from their regular living area. Perhaps that place may be your garage, an extra room, the basement, or even outdoors. Wherever it is, I suggest it be a place that has lots of sunlight or is brightly lit, since we tend to respond better to brighter places than dark and dreary ones.

I would also suggest that you stay there until you're finished working out. That means you should bring all the water you'll need during your workout to your workout area. It is just too easy to get distracted if you're working out downstairs or in the garage and halfway through you need to leave for a glass of water. Any number of things could distract you from getting back to your workout—the phone ringing, something on TV, or people (children, spouses, friends, etc.) stopping you for "just a minute" of your time.

Finally, if you share your home with others, you need to let it be known that you are not to be interrupted in any way while you are working out. This is your time that you're taking for your body, to do something that makes you look and feel good.

If you live alone, then you need to turn off the phone, turn the answering machine volume down to zero, shut off the TV, and ignore the doorbell. Do not pay attention to anything else while you are working out.

You'll find it very helpful if you put yourself on a regular training schedule. Your body thrives on regularity in sleep and meals, and it's the same with exercise. Give your body the exercise it needs—at regular times throughout the week—and you'll find it very easy to stay with your workout program.

Whether you train at home or in a gym, you should always do something differently. Never do the same workout twice—even if that only means changing the order of your favorite exercises but keeping the same workout, which I advise not to always do.

People get bored very quickly. And really, just how fun is it to do the same workout, week after week, at home, by yourself? Heck, even the most excited workout people would get bored with that

pretty quickly.

Try new things. If you see something in a magazine or book that looks and sounds pretty cool, then try it and see if it works for you. Change not only the exercises and the order that you do them, but also change the number of sets and reps, the weight used, the angles you use them, alternate between fast reps, slow reps, full reps, partial reps, longer workouts, shorter workouts, and on and on.

Just do something different; make your workout time and place your little oasis away from the distractions of your everyday living and have lots of fun doing it. Find things that keep you excited and do them, and your workout will be filled with excitement!

Accurately Assessing Your Success/Progress

So, how do you know when you're making progress? The first way is to ask yourself how you feel. If you're feeling better about yourself and your body, then you're doing something right and making progress.

The next step would be to accurately assess how you look. And don't use the scale to do it. If you put too much emphasis on achieving a certain number—as in losing or gaining weight (remember the majority of scales tell you how much weight and not *fat* that you've lost)—then much of how you feel about yourself and your progress will be tied into what the scale tells you. And the scale can be a real liar at times, since it doesn't tell you the changing composition of your body but only the number of pounds it weighs.

As you know, muscle weighs more than fat, and if your body is changing and losing the fat and adding a bit of lean, healthy muscle tissue, you can actually be looking and feeling better and weighing more! But, if you are just paying attention to how much you weigh, then the added

weight might really bum you out and steal your motivation, and you will lose your inspiration to keep working out.

To really get a good indication of how your body is changing (and it will, believe me), use a mirror. The mirror doesn't care about numbers and how much you weigh. It simply reflects back to you what you look like at that given moment of the day. And your body can change greatly from hour to hour and day to day due to hormones, sleep, food and fluid intake, water retention, and so on. So if you must look in the mirror, then try doing it at different times on different days to see how your body changes.

The other feedback method is to use a pair of old tight-fitting pants. If you're still having problems getting them on, then you've got a bit more work to do. If the pants are getting easier to slip on or getting loose, then you're on the right track. Be careful of using just any kind of pants, especially jeans that have just been washed and dried; they can shrink up and make you think you're heavier than you really are.

Remember that working out is something that will make you look and feel good, and it will be something you'll want to do for the rest of your life. You can shape your body, and your body will respond if you just do the right things for it. Do them regularly and be patient.

LIFE LESSON

VERY FEW PEOPLE SEE LIFE AS YOU DO

We are all born under the same sky,
but we don't all have the same horizon.

—Konrad Adenaur

Amazing how we want others to see things as we see them. Ever notice how downright frustrating it can be when they don't? Inside of us, our true personality wants to come out; yet there's no way we feel safe in letting it unless we feel that others really understand us.

The truth is, that's not going to happen. Why? Because each of us will see the same events and experiences differently. One reason could be that each of our brains is wired differently. It's true; even twins see events and remember experiences differently.

Another big reason is that our filter, which everything must first pass through, is colored by our perceptions about what has happened to us in the past and what we have chosen to keep as important references for any future events that we might experience. The brain is always looking for a past event to relate to whatever new experience it may be seeing and experiencing now.

Admit it. Wouldn't it be great if others could step inside our bodies for only a brief few seconds to feel those things we're feeling? To know why we want to change how we look and feel, instead of finding fault or reasons why we can't?

THE LESSON TO BE LEARNED

Since others will never totally understand you, the best you can do is try to understand the other person's reference system. Learn how they describe their experiences. Once you understand their reference system, then work on describing to them the things you want—such as making nutritional and exercise changes—with the words, pictures, or emotions they understand best.

Have them do the same for you. Get on the same wavelength. Be specific about your descriptions and what you want them to know. A support team can be invaluable as you begin the road to a new you.

THOUSANDS UPON THOUSANDS OF
PERSONS HAVE STUDIED DISEASE.
ALMOST NO ONE HAS STUDIED HEALTH.

—ADELLE DAVIS,
LET'S EAT RIGHT TO KEEP FIT

Part II: Nutrition

CHAPTER 5

NUTRITION OVERVIEW

We could talk for days about nutrition. Most people know if they are eating well or not and are often surprised at how well they know what things are good for their bodies and what things aren't.

The big thing about nutrition that people always ask me about is supplements. Which to take, which not take, the latest incredible pill or powder, and so on.

Lots of people swear by supplements, and some of these products do have their place in your

food pantry, but most do not.

You need to understand that supplements are (as the word says), *a supplement to something*. They are designed to work along with a good, nutritious eating plan. Supplements will not make up for poor eating habits, no matter what kind you use or how many you take.

Your body needs the nutrients from a variety of foods, such as grains, meats, dairy products, vegetables, and fruits. Your body was built and designed to use these foods as your primary fuel and nutrient sources. Yet somewhere along the way, our lives got too busy, and the message from many supplement makers got blurred.

Over the years, the top-level athletes I've worked with and the scientists and researchers I've spoken to have said:

- Supplements may work for some people, but not nearly as well for others.
- In people for whom supplements do work, many report only *minimal* differences in performance.

- A smaller number of these people may notice a real change in performance, but one that usually only lasts a short time and can be quite expensive to maintain.
- When you look at the cost-to-performance /results ratio, supplements are expensive.
- Many people say they have to take supplements often and in high dosages—even higher than what the magazines tell you—in order to get any noticeable results.
- Your money is more wisely spent by buying good, healthy foods.

Water and Food

Your body likes to be fed and watered frequently throughout the day. It will respond much better to a balanced steady diet than it will to missed meals, lack of water, or the overloading of food and water when you have the time.

Never let thirst be the signal to drink a glass of water; it is too late by then. Your body needs to drink at least eight to twelve glasses of water per day. This translates to an average of roughly sixty-four ounces of water per day just for normal body function.

If you're working out, staying active, are busy

> **BONUSES TO DRINKING MORE WATER**
> - Your body will have all the water it needs.
> - Your skin will look better.
> - Water helps in fat metabolism (i.e., it helps your body use fat more efficiently).
> - Your body won't hold water or bloat you due to not getting enough water.
> - Your muscles (body) look and perform better. Researchers have found that for every 1 percent drop in fluid in your body (from not getting enough water), there can be a 10 percent decrease in muscle strength.

all the time, especially in hot weather, your body needs *much more* than sixty-four ounces.

I'll make it easy for you. Drink enough water to match your bodyweight. If you weigh 150 pounds, drink 150 ounces per day. No, you don't drink it all at one time. Drink the 150 ounces throughout the entire day, morning through night. Your body also responds well to eating smaller meals instead of those big gut-busters at lunch or dinner—especially if it is a late dinner. This means eating about every three hours or so. Hey, don't panic when I say eat every three hours, I'm talking about eating small, nutritious meals and snacks.

Now, here's where supplements can help. I know you're busy, probably too busy to cook every meal, but even though fast-food places would be easier and they would love to see you coming in, there's a more nutritious way.

Enter the meal replacement protein shake. Lots of companies sell them, and if you use them right, they actually work very well. What could be quicker than to tear open a packet, pour it into a blender with water, juice, or milk (for a change of pace you could add a banana or strawberries, maybe a little ice), and voilà! You now have a good-for-you nutritious meal that you can take with you on the go.

That's one of the ways supplements can work for you. The other is taking a good multivitamin/mineral with perhaps some additional antioxidant like vitamin C. You should think of vitamins and minerals as the sparkplugs your body engine needs in order to use the food you eat for all those incredible bodily functions (i.e., digestion, breathing, healing, recuperation, etc.).

Granted, if you're eating great fresh foods and getting the right quantities, many nay-sayers will question the need for using vitamins and minerals, and they have a point. However, how many people do you know who have well-balanced meals every day and can look at their eating habits and tell you it's textbook all the way? Not very many.

So, give yourself a little easy insurance and take a multivitamin/mineral supplement in the morning at breakfast and another at night during dinner. You also might want to add in some extra vitamin C with that.

You don't need to buy the expensive kind either. The late, two-time Nobel Prize winner and noted vitamin C researcher Dr. Linus Pauling told me the cheap kinds work just as well.

Now let's talk a little about what to eat. Variety is the word to remember here. You don't want to do what so many people try to do and eat the same few favorite foods week after week after week; it will get very boring.

Mix things up. Try new things, new varieties. Give your body new foods and see how you feel and how your body responds to those foods. Just like training, it will do your body good to try new and different things.

Which Should I Eat—Protein, Carbohydrates, or Fat?

How about all of them! Within reason and the right ratios, carbohydrates are the fuel your body uses the fastest. You've heard of glucose? Well, your body breaks down the carbohydrates you eat into glucose. Then the glucose is stored in your muscles and liver as glycogen, and that is the fuel your body can easily and quickly use for workouts and other activities.

Here's something many people don't know. That amazing body of yours will use the food source you give it most as its primary source of energy.

For example, if you eat a lot of fat, your body will use more fat for fuel; if it's carbohydrates, then carbohydrates will be used as glycogen for the fuel source. But both are not used equally efficiently or effectively.

Remember earlier when I mentioned about getting a balance of nutrients? Too much of one means there won't be enough room for the others, and too much of the wrong one can really cut into your body's workout fuel and recovery fuel.

When eating carbohydrates, try to get a balance of roughly 50 percent from fast-burning simple sugars such as fruit, juice, and honey; and the other 50 percent from slow-burning complex carbs such as vegetables, beans, grains, pasta, legumes, and brown rice.

Let's Talk about Protein

Working out increases your body's need for nutrients, and if you're working out hard, you're going to need more protein than someone who is not as active. Try to get between 0.7 to 1.3 grams per pound of bodyweight per day.

For example, a 130-pound person should eat anywhere from 91 to 130 grams of protein a day. A 175-pound person would need 122.5 to 175 grams of protein, and a 225-pound person should have 157.5 to 225 grams of protein per day. Start with the lower number for your bodyweight and slowly adjust the protein upward each week, only if your body needs it.

I'm still amazed at how many people still believe the myth that the body can use only 20–50 grams of protein at a time. The scientists and researchers I've talked to say that they have yet to see a conclusive study that proves this.

The bottom line is that your body type, age, metabolism, genetics, activity level, and intensity level all determine how much protein your body will need at any given time, so you should experiment and find what intake level is best for you.

Of all the nutrients you eat, carbohydrates are protein sparing. Meaning, your body will use carbohydrates as its primary fuel before tapping into your body's protein reserves. And that's what you want, because you want as much protein as possible to be utilized by your body for tissue repair and recovery.

Aim for getting your protein from lean meat, skinless chicken and turkey, fish, egg whites, nonfat dairy, skim milk powder, or high-quality whey or soy proteins.

Those Things Called Electrolytes

Electrolytes are electrically charged ions produced by your body when the mineral salts in your body are dissolved in water. But you don't need to know all the science to understand that the two biggest electrolytes in your body are potassium and sodium. These electrolytes help the body deliver nutrients (along with wastes) across cell membranes. Your body quickly loses electrolytes whenever you're physically active. You can quickly and simply replace those electrolytes by drinking a sports drink, but you can also just eat more of the things you already use. For example, to replace sodium and chloride, add a little extra salt to your food. To replace potassium, have some fruits likes oranges and bananas.

Preworkout Fuel

One size doesn't fit all when it comes to what to eat and not eat before exercising. Some folks believe that eating a meal loaded with complex carbohydrates (like pasta) the night before you train loads the body with plenty of energy for the next day.

Many others say that the meal roughly two or so hours before your activity is what makes the difference. For me, I've found it to be a combination of the two plus two other variables: the amount of activity performed the week before and the overall composition of the diet for that week.

Interestingly, I've found that if I worked out and was physically active for at least three or four days that week, the regular and extra calories ingested during my meals seemed to be primarily used for recuperation, repair, and growth from the previous exercise I put my body through, with little left over for additional physical demands.

Yet, on the weeks that I cut back on the intensity of my training and kept my complex carbohydrate intake at 50 percent, protein at 35 percent, and fat at 15 percent, I found that my body had plenty of energy and endurance for whatever activity/sport I was doing.

Just keep in mind that you, me, and everyone else are going to respond differently to how our bodies use foods and the different compositions of carbohydrate, protein, and fats in our diets.

Try to eat small meals throughout the day, about three to four hours apart. Small meals won't overtax your body's ability to digest and assimilate the nutrients that will allow your body to better use those nutrients with minimal waste. Small meals will keep your blood sugar levels stable all day, and they give your body the ratio of proper nutrients it needs at the times and amounts it can optimally use them.

Eat clean to be lean. For the most part, a leaner athlete (within reason) can be a more effective athlete. Excess body fat slows you down and takes up space, and, unlike muscle, fat is not living tissue. Lean muscle tissue is living tissue (it needs nutrients to feed it), and the more you have—within reason—the more of those nutritious foods you can eat.

Frequent, smaller meals, along with the extra calories your lean tissue needs, help to create a metabolic boost that will then help your body burn calories more efficiently. Some people say all of these things help their body to burn body fat

SOME GREAT BREAKFAST CHOICES

- Cottage cheese (nonfat or low-fat) and fruit
- Yogurt mixed with muesli, bran, or high-fiber cereal
- Eggs with grapefruit and unbuttered whole-grain bread
- High-fiber/low-fat cereal with skim milk
- Fresh juice with bagels
- Oatmeal mixed and cooked with skim milk, honey, and sliced banana fortified with extra skim milk powder

SOME GREAT LUNCH CHOICES

- Dark green salad with tuna (in spring water), turkey, or chicken, and piece of fruit
- Tuna or egg white salad (made with nonfat mayo, sweet relish, chili powder, celery salt, celery) with nonfat or low-fat wholegrain crackers, piece of fruit
- Bagel with low-fat chicken or tuna salad spread and a piece of fruit

more effectively. Sort of best of both worlds: eat more calories, lose more fat.

However, always keep in mind that the numero uno thing to remember about losing body fat is the total amount of calories you are eating in a day versus the total number of calories you are burning in a day. Don't be overly concerned about whether you're eating the right ratio of nutrients, eating them at the right time, etcetera. The bottom line is: if you're eating more food than you can use, you're going to get fat.

Always have a good breakfast and never miss this meal. Choose a different kind of breakfast every day. Always have a glass of water upon waking and about twenty to thirty minutes before a meal so it won't interfere with digestion.

During meals, only sip your water. Drinking too much water with meals tends to dilute important stomach acids needed for the breakdown of nutrients from the food.

Eating after Training

I'd like to briefly tell you about a very important time for you to refuel your body. So important in fact, that many fitness experts and researchers believe it may be the most important meal of the day: It's right after you work out.

Some research has shown that the body will store muscle fuel (glycogen) nearly *twice as effectively* in a brief period right after exercise (within about forty minutes) as at other times throughout the day when there was no exercise. And some research has also shown that the body will store as much as twice the amount of glycogen from sucrose and glucose as from fructose.

I recommend a twelve-ounce can of fruit juice for this refueling fuel. You might want to dilute the fruit juice with some water, as many athletes say this has helped their bodies make better use of the carbs. Try it both ways and see what works best for you.

SOME GREAT DINNER CHOICES AND SIDE DISHES

- Fish, lean beef, skinless chicken, or turkey
- Pasta (with red sauce, low-fat white sauce, or plain)
- Dark green leafy and fibrous vegetables
- White fibrous vegetables (cauliflower)
- Richly colored vegetables (tomatoes, squash, peppers, etc.)

SOME GREAT SNACK CHOICES

- Fruit
- Celery, carrots
- Popcorn (no butter)
- Bagels
- Rice cakes with applesauce
- Beef or turkey jerky

LIFE LESSON

LIFE IS MEANT TO BE ENJOYED, NOT ENDURED

Very little is needed to make a happy life.
It is all within yourself, in your way of thinking.

—Marcus Aurelius

Who said that life was meant to be a struggle, to be difficult and unpleasant? Who said that exercise was a chore? Getting yourself back in shape and changing how you look and feel is so good for you it can't feel bad. Who filled our minds with this garbage? Forget about what others think. Do you really believe life was meant to be endured, not enjoyed? Well, I've got some news for you.

Somewhere along the way people developed a morbid sense of satisfaction and reward from struggle. Deep inside of them, they have this belief that the harder life is, the bigger the reward they will get down the road. After all, everyone around seems to be struggling, so it must mean you should too, right?

THE LESSON TO BE LEARNED

This is absolutely not true! The fun of life is getting the payoff on your own terms. The fact is, *you can have anything in life you truly desire once you give up the belief that you can't have it.* This includes changing how you look and feel.

Change the way you see your life into a fun game. Treat each day as a wonderful surprise and an incredible experience to learn from. Use each surprise and experience to help you grow and become bigger, better, and more in control of your life. Develop and cultivate an awareness like never before, and you will achieve whatever it is you truly desire.

Most people allow themselves to be troubled and hurt by many things; this allows others to steal the very happiness and joy from them. *Limiting beliefs create limiting results, which create unsatisfying and very limited lives.*

The point is, *change your thinking and you change your life.* There is no faster or easier way to do it. Once you do, it'll be something you'll enjoy for the rest of your life.

CHAPTER 6

POWERFUL EATING STRATEGIES: THE ZIGZAG PRINCIPLE

Looking for an incredibly easy way to burn fat, be leaner, and have more energy that will allow you to eat more food? You've found it! Zigzagging. "Zigzagging? What the heck is that?" It's simply changing the amount and kind of food you eat each day. One day you eat more; the next day you eat less. So easy and so effective.

You see, your body can become very stagnant—it wants to stay right where it is and the condition it's in—especially if you're always eating the same foods in the same proportions at the same time each day.

This tendency of your body to remain the same is called homeostasis. All you need to know is that once your body gets used to doing the same thing over and over, it doesn't want to change, and it will resist if you try to make it. That is, unless you learn how to zigzag.

You've no doubt felt the effects of this; your body weight tends to stay the same, and it's hard as heck for you to make any lasting changes—either up or down—in your body weight number

or in your appearance.

That's why so many people, out of frustration, resort to drastic measures to change how much they weigh. And therein lies the problem: all they seem to care about is losing weight rather than losing fat. I can show you how to lose lots of weight in a hurry—like five pounds in forty-eight hours—but all you would be doing is losing water weight and not fat.

I want you to get this "I wanna lose weight" idea out of your mind. Focusing on losing weight and wanting to get down to some magical weight number will not solve your problem. It also will not quench your desire to have a new body, look good, and feel great.

The majority of people who lose weight end up losing very little fat, yet lose lots of lean muscle tissue. This is a major no-no. Fat just sits there and takes up space on your body. It slows you down, keeps you sluggish, and makes you look like someone you'd rather not look like.

What you want is lean muscle tissue. Muscle is living tissue, and it needs food every day to live.

Fat does not. Because muscle is living tissue, you can eat more—you've got to feed that muscle—and you'll still weigh less. Lean muscle tissue creates a metabolic response (fires up the energy furnace inside your body) that actually causes your body to burn fat just to keep the flame inside the furnace burning hot.

Did you hear that? As you develop muscle, your body will require more fuel; you can eat more and your body will use that food more efficiently. That is, as long as you're giving your body the right kinds of protein, carbohydrates, and fat that it needs, in the right proportions, throughout the day.

Let me paint a vivid picture for you. Imagine you are a person who weighs 145 pounds, and you want to keep all the muscle you can but lose the fat. Now imagine you have a friend who is the same height and weighs 145 pounds, just like you. However, all your friend cares about is losing weight and getting to a certain weight number.

You begin to work out using *Home Bodybuilding* and your friend begins by using the latest weight-loss drug or starving herself, like she always has. Now, both of you stand in front of a mirror. Be prepared, because both of you are about to experience a big surprise.

Your reflection shows a body that's lean, firm, and has great shape. Your friend's reflection shows a body that's flabby, bulky, and still looks out of shape. But you ask, how can that be, especially when you both weigh the same?

The difference lies in the *composition* of your bodies, not how much you weigh. You see, your friend was focused only on reaching a weight number and didn't care about eating or exercising correctly. By doing this her metabolism slowed down, because the diet drugs and/or severely limited food intake curbed her appetite. This caused her to not eat the right amount of protein, carbohydrates, and fat that preserves lean muscle tissue

and keeps the metabolic fire burning. She wasn't eating enough protein, but her body still needed it. So where do you think it got it from? Her muscles. Yeah, lean tissue. Why? Because muscle is made up of protein. In other words, her body fed upon itself (the lean muscle tissue made up of protein) just so it could get the nutrients it needed when it needed them. When that happened, muscle was replaced with fat.

If your friend only knew the simple nutritional and exercise tips you're learning, she'd quickly and easily have the answers and results she so desperately wants, without using drugs, diets, and other gimmicks.

Keeping your muscle is very important to you. Remember what we just talked about: The more muscle you have, the more you can eat, because your metabolism—the furnace inside you that burns food—is burning hot. Muscle is living tissue that needs food, and food keeps your furnace going. When your body is getting the right balance of proteins, carbohydrates, and fats, the furnace starts burning your excess fat, and not the protein from your lean muscle tissue or those protein-saving nutrients such as carbohydrates.

Talk about a great new look. Your body will look lean and firm because you gave it the nutrients (proteins, carbohydrates, and fats) it needed throughout the day, in the right ratio it needed them. The end result is that you can weigh the same as your friend, but you look 100 percent better because you're leaner and have more muscle.

Right here and right now, let's do one thing; throw away your scale, or at least put it away for awhile. You see, the scale can be a saboteur to your nutritional and fitness goals. If you live by the scale, you'll constantly be frustrated by the scale.

What scales will never tell you is how you actually look and the composition of your body. That is, how much of what you weigh is fat and how much of it is muscle. So, let's put the scale away and just let the mirror and your clothes be the guides.

Are You Ready to Zigzag?

Okay, by now you should know that keeping your muscle and losing excess fat is the goal. You just

learned that eating the right portions of protein, carbs, and fat is a very important way to do that. But I'm about to show you a little something extra that is very simple and very effective.

One of the strangest things about being able to lose fat (yes, of course, that means you'll lose weight) and keep lean muscle tissue is that you need to keep your body off balance. Never allow your body to get used to one thing. You always want to keep it guessing what in the heck you're going to do to it next. Strangely enough, this kind of surprise attack actually helps keep your body in

balance! You got that? *Throw it off balance to keep it in balance.* And when it comes to eating, zigzagging is one very effective way to do it. Here's how:

- For seven days write down what you eat each day, including snacks.

- Once you have done this for seven days, go to any local bookstore and pick up a copy of a food-count book. This kind of book lists nearly every food and gives you the breakdown of calories, fat, protein, carbohydrates, and so on for those foods. I highly recommend *The Book of Food Counts* by Corinne Netzer.

- Get out your seven-day list of foods you've eaten and write down the number of calories for each food. For example, let's say you had a five-ounce piece of chicken breast. You simply look up chicken in the book, look for the approximate serving size you had (unless you have a food scale, then just estimate the best you can), and find the total number of calories for that size chicken breast; you will probably see a number like 140 calories.

- Add up the numbers for all seven days to get your total number of calories consumed for the week. For example, let's say your seven-day total comes to 21,000 calories. That's 3,000 calories a day times seven days = 21,000 calories. Easy.

- Now you have the two numbers you need to start zigzagging; the daily average total (3,000 calories) and the weekly total (21,000 calories).

- Using our 3,000 calorie per day example, here's how you'll zigzag:

1. Day one eat 2,700 calories
2. Day two eat 3,300 calories
3. Day three eat 2,000 calories

4. Day four eat 4,000 calories
5. Day five eat 3,500 calories
6. Day six eat 2,500 calories
7. Day seven eat 3,000 calories

By simply changing how much food you eat each day, you never eat the same amount of food two days in a row. Some days you eat a lot of calories, but it's the same 21,000 per week that you were eating before! You don't eat a single calorie more than you did before, but it's how you eat those calories that causes incredible changes in your body. By shocking your body and throwing it off balance, you never give your body a chance to adapt to what you were doing. And you know what else happens? You also cause your body's food furnace to burn even hotter, which helps your body burn fat and burn it more effectively. You do all that just by changing how much you eat every day. You don't even have to run, walk, or work out to do it. Now that's pretty cool.

Here's how zigzagging works. Because you eat more calories one day and fewer the next, you throw your body off balance; it doesn't know how many calories it is going to get the next meal, let alone the next day.

When that happens, to overcompensate for the surprise, your body's metabolism—the furnace that burns food—becomes faster and hotter, thereby allowing you to burn more calories, eat more food, and burn fat and do it faster than ever before because you use the food you eat more efficiently.

Best of all, you do it naturally—without any drugs or dieting—and *you can even do it without exercise!* However, if you want super-incredible results in a hurry, add a little exercise, like the kind I'm about to show you, and you'll be there in no time.

Zigzagging works great when you not only vary the quantity of food eaten each day, but also vary the kinds of food you eat each meal. *Always change what you eat, when you eat, and how much you eat, each and every day.* Make this a rule for life.

And if you want to lose the fat even faster, slowly reduce your caloric intake each week. Many people make the mistake of changing too many things too quickly, not really ever knowing the one factor that was responsible for their fat loss.

Was it the fifty calories a day they cut out? Was it more exercise? Was it more protein and fewer carbs? Unless you slowly adjust one variable at a time and give it enough time to see how it works, you'll never know what your body responds best to.

That's why reducing your calories little by little works so well for people. By keeping their activity level and everything else in their life the same, when they change only one variable at a time—like reducing the amount of food they eat each day by fifty or so calories—they have precise control over what that fifty-calorie reduction does or does not do to their body.

Once you find the perfect daily/weekly amount of calories for your body, then it's a breeze to pick another variable—such as exercise—and change it a bit to see how that affects you. The thing to remember is to take your time and give your body enough time so it can adjust to any change and give you accurate feedback.

A good rule of thumb: *Try to eat your biggest meal in the morning or very early in the day and gradually reduce the amount of food you eat during each meal as the day goes on.* If breakfast has always been tough for you to eat, then have your biggest meal of the day as early in the day as possible.

And because many people's metabolism runs faster during the early part of the day, they find that their body is quite forgiving and will more effectively burn any excess calories they eat if they eat those excess calories early enough in the day. Bottom line: Unless you've got a racehorse metabolism, stay away from those late-night gut-buster meals!

Here's a very important thing to remember. *When it comes to how much food you should eat at a meal, always try to eat each meal based on what your activity level will be for the next two to three hours and not on what you've already done.* Not doing this is a huge mistake that people make.

For example, if you're planning some physical activity like a workout, walk, or run, then you should consume more calories an hour or so before the activity than you would after that workout or physical activity. That way you'll have plenty of fuel for the activity. Even though it's important to refuel after exercise, you should eat more before you're active and less after the activity is finished.

One other thing zigzagging does is work incredibly well for women with PMS (Premenstrual Syndrome). During those some-times "difficult" days, many women's bodies crave all kinds of foods and in quantities they normally wouldn't crave during the rest of the month. If this describes you, that's okay. Go ahead and give your body whatever it craves, whenever it craves it. Just don't do it for more than a few days in a row. You should also adjust your eating schedule to reflect those extra calories and cravings by making those meals and days you eat more your high zigzag day. That is, those will be the days that your daily calorie intake will be fairly high. Then in a day or so, when your body reduces its craving, lower your food intake so your daily calories will be fewer. These will be your low zigzag days.

By simply adjusting your high- and low-calorie days, you will still be eating the same exact number of calories for the week. Just make sure you don't go over that weekly total number. If we're using the 21,000-calorie number for the week, you always want to stay at that number or slightly below it.

In addition to the incredible results you're going to experience using zigzagging, the other great thing is that, before you know it, you won't have to keep count of your foods anymore.

Very quickly, you'll be amazed at just how fast your mind and body will instinctively know just how much or little you should eat at any given meal. Like a finely tuned machine, your body will tell you when to eat, what to eat, and when to stop. Your body's been trying to talk to you all these years. Now, you're about to listen.

Finally, I want you to do yourself and me a big favor and start treating yourself better and not be so darn hard on yourself. For heaven's sake, be your own best friend.

You see, whenever you have cravings for certain foods, there's never any need to freak out (stop eating or do hours of cardio workouts) or do anything drastic. Just give your body whatever it wants, when it wants it, and adjust—either less or more—how much food you eat the next day. If you ate a lot today, then don't eat as much tomorrow. So simple. In the end, it'll all balance out, and zigzagging will always keep you on target.

LIFE LESSON

YOU CAN ALWAYS DO THINGS MUCH BETTER AND FASTER THAN YOU THINK YOU CAN

*If we were to do all that we are capable of doing,
we would literally astonish ourselves.*

—Thomas A. Edison

We're experts at putting limits on our dreams and abilities. People will state their limitations without your even asking. But ask them to tell you about their potential and possibilities and see how the experience becomes difficult for them.

Maybe you're one of these people? If so, ask yourself why have you let the limiting and constricting beliefs of family, friends, and society hold you down? Why is it that you've concentrated so much on what you can't do, how you can't change your body and life? Why haven't you focused on all the things you can do?

The truth is, your potential is unlimited. That's right, without any limits. And if that's the case, which it is, then why haven't you allowed yourself to do the things you truly want to do and see just how fast your engine will run?

THE LESSON TO BE LEARNED

Think back to a time when you were really challenged to achieve a goal or get a job done—something that seemed nearly impossible—and you did it beyond your own and anyone else's expectations. You pushed yourself out of the rut, went beyond your comfort zone, and achieved more than you ever thought possible.

It was an incredible feeling wasn't it? You can have that same kind experience every day, in any area of your life, if you will only push yourself just a little more.

Your body is the most incredible machine ever designed, and it begs to be worked out— physically, mentally, and spiritually—every single day. If you keep pushing it past what it's used to, you will find that it always responds.

Each time you push yourself and expect more from yourself than what you're used to, your body and mind respond beautifully by giving you that which you are asking for.

Always know that your capacity and ability to experience and do better things, greater things, is unlimited. *You have so much awesome power.* All you've got to do is use it.

I DO NOT KNOW WHAT I MAY APPEAR
TO THE WORLD, BUT TO MYSELF
I SEEM TO HAVE ONLY BEEN LIKE
A BOY PLAYING ON THE SEASHORE,
AND DIVERTING MYSELF IN NOW AND
THEN FINDING A PRETTIER SHELL,
OR SMOOTHER PEBBLE THAN ORDINARY,
WHILST THE GREAT OCEAN OF TRUTH
LAY ALL UNDISCOVERED BEFORE ME.

—SIR ISAAC NEWTON

Part III: The Basics

CHAPTER 7

SAFETY AND INJURIES

B esides the obvious safety precaution of warming up before, during, and after exercise, there are a few other guidelines I'd like you to follow when it comes to training at home.

Let Others Know You Are Training

This could be as simple as saying, "Hey, I'm going to work out," if you're living in a house with others. Or leave a note on the kitchen table, on the door, or someplace where others will see it. Letting people know you're working out is just a little safety measure, especially if you're just starting out and getting used to it all.

Check All Equipment Before Working Out

Equipment is equipment, and things get loose, break, or wear out when they are used, so give all of your equipment a good once-over before working out.

Consider airplanes and pilots. Before each flight, the pilot walks around the plane, usually with a flashlight in hand, and visually checks the aircraft for anything that looks out of place. That's what I want you to do; check your equipment.

What should you look for? Here's a list:

- Loose or missing bolts, nuts, and screws
- Broken, frayed, or loose cables
- Stripped and loose cable connections to weights, through pulleys and connection devices such as snaps, clips, or other fastening devices
- Bent, wobbly, or cracked pulleys
- Loose seats and benches
- Broken or loose weights
- Loose or broken collars on barbells and dumbbells
- Cracked, broken, or slipping and loose belts on treadmills
- Loose or broken chains, belts, or gears on bikes and stair steppers
- Cracked and loose pedals on bikes and stair steppers
- Any squeaky moving parts on any machine, barbells, or dumbbells

If they are not worn out or broken, then be sure to lubricate your equipment parts at least once a week.

Injuries: How to Avoid Them and What to Do If You Have One

Over the years, I've met many people who'd been injured and who could have avoided their injuries if only they would've listened to the wisdom of their bodies. Instead, thinking they know better, they ignored the body's warning signals, and they paid the price.

Your body is absolutely amazing in its ability to get stronger, adapt, recover, renew, replenish, and repair itself. It's when we think we know the healing and living processes better than our bodies that we get into trouble.

Many people are driven to achieve a new look and will do so at almost any cost, even if it means injury. For many reasons, these people feel that their whole self-image, who they are as a person, is dependent upon how they look, and nothing could be further from the truth.

Resting one's self-image and self-esteem on such a shaky foundation is bound to cause inner turmoil whenever you decide that you look too fat or too thin today, or that you're flabby here and not firm enough there. You ate too much last night, so you starve yourself today to make up for it. You go on and on; the list is endless, and so is the pain when you do that.

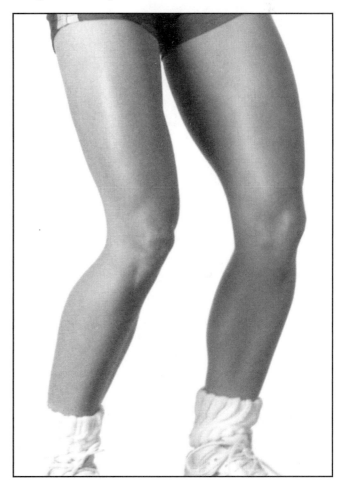

Common Injury Areas

The injuries I see and hear about most affect:

- Knees
- Elbows
- Shoulders
- Wrists
- Neck

So pay careful attention to these and any other areas you think could be vulnerable. Following are a few commonsense rules that will help.

RULES TO AVOID COMMON INJURIES

Rule #1

Make time to warm up before, during, and after training.

Rule #2

Go slow and steady. Use good exercise form and be consistent.

Rule #3

If at any time you feel something that is painful (you'll be able to differentiate between good, old-fashioned making-the-muscles-work kind of discomfort, which is normal, and real pain), stop immediately and don't do that exercise. Stretch some more, then try another exercise; if the pain persists, cool down and take a break.

Rule #4

Allow your body to rest completely and heal that injury. Even if many days have passed, if you can still feel a slight twinge or ache, continue to rest. If you feel the pain, then do not train!

Rule #5

Once you have returned to 100 percent, begin very slowly by moving that body part with no weights. Start with a very limited range of motion and slowly and gradually increase the range of motion until it is 100 percent normal.

Rule #6

Once it is 100 percent normal and you feel no pain or discomfort, begin to add a very light set of an exercise for that body part that is easy and comfortable for you to do. For example, if you have a shoulder injury, that means no behind-the-neck barbell shoulder presses. Instead, do no-weight or lightweight movements, such as holding a barbell plate (2½, 5, or 10 pounds) or doing dumbbell lateral-type movements. Focus on doing any kind of exercise that allows for the freest range of movement and ones that will allow you to find the right and best-feeling exercise groove for you and your body.

Rule #7

Next workout, add another weight set of that exercise. Each workout, slowly add another weight exercise until you're back to the level you were before the injury. Add weight, sets, reps, and exercises slowly and stop immediately if you feel *any* pain.

Rule #8

Include a new segment to your workout that includes more emphasis on stretching, increasing range of motion, and warm-ups for any body parts or areas that might be sensitive.

Rule #9

Take at least one week off from training for every four to six weeks of training you do. Even if you're making great progress, feeling no injuries, no pain, no discomfort, or no anything else, take the time off. Force yourself, if you have to, to take the time off. It will do amazing things for your body, attitude, and results.

CHAPTER 8

WORKOUT STRUCTURES

How to work out is one of the biggest causes of confusion for people.

I'm going to give you some good guidelines to follow, and then, depending on your goals, experience, and time you have to work out, you can choose what kind of workout you'd like to do.

In the pages that follow these workout structures tips, you'll find lots of different exercises to choose from for all of your body parts. Try them all, one by one, but not during the same week, and see which ones work best for you. Find at least two or more exercises for each body part. Then use one or two of them each time you work out. Remember to alternate the order and combination each time

Even if you're using only a few exercises that you've found work best for your body, never do the same thing twice!

The Four Stages of Training
Stage One—Freshman Level

FRESHMAN SCHEDULE

Monday = entire body
Tuesday = rest
Wednesday = entire body
Thursday = rest
Friday = entire body
Saturday = rest
Sunday = rest

This stage requires little or no training experience or could be used when coming back from a layoff.

The foundation for the beginner workout is to work your entire body, once every other day (i.e., Monday-Wednesday-Friday), three times per week. Some people like a Tuesday-Thursday-Saturday or a Wednesday-Friday-Sunday schedule better; it's your choice. Decide which days are best based on your lifestyle and schedule.

On the days you don't work out, let your body recuperate from the previous day's workout.

Follow these guidelines:

- Pick only one or two exercises per body part.
- Do one to three sets per exercise per body part.
- Rest one minute between sets and three to five minutes between body parts.
- Do eight to twelve reps for upper body.
- Do twelve to twenty reps for lower body.

Stay on the beginner program for at least ninety days before doing any other kind of workout.

Stage Two—Sophomore Level

SOPHOMORE SCHEDULE

Monday = upper body
Tuesday = lower body
Wednesday = rest
Thursday = upper body
Friday = lower body
Saturday = rest
Sunday = rest

After at least ninety days on the beginner program, you're ready to move to the next level, stage two. In this stage, you'll be adding more exercises, sets, and reps and will be decreasing rest times, thereby allowing you to do more in relatively the same period of time.

The biggest change will be that you'll only be working your entire body two times a week, instead of three like you did on the stage one beginner program. You will do this by splitting your workouts for the whole body into two days, instead of having to do all of it in one day.

For example, you will work half your body on Monday and the other half on Tuesday, then take Wednesday off and come back on Thursday and Friday and do your second whole-body workout

for that week.

You might want to do upper body on Monday and legs and calves on Tuesday. Or you might want to do a push/pull type of program where you'd do chest, shoulders, and triceps on Monday and legs, back, and biceps on Tuesday. Feel free to change days around to what fits your schedule best. Just make sure you do two days of workouts, take one day off, do two more days of workouts, then take two days off (like the weekend if you're doing the Monday/Tuesday—Thursday/Friday routine).

Follow these guidelines:

- Do two to three exercises per body part.
- Do two to three sets per exercise per body part (i.e., six to nine sets per body part).
- Rest forty-five seconds between sets and two to three minutes between body parts.
- Do five to nine reps for upper body.
- Do twelve to thirty reps for lower body.

Stay on the stage-two program for at least ninety days before doing any other kind of workout.

Stage Three—Junior Level

JUNIOR SCHEDULE

Monday = partial upper body
Tuesday = lower body
Wednesday = partial upper body
Thursday = rest
Friday, Saturday, Sunday = repeat sequence

As you progress and your body gets stronger/leaner/bigger/smaller, you're going to find that your ability to generate higher workout intensity will increase. This means it will take you less time to make your muscles—and body—work harder.

As you improve, your workout focus will begin to shift from doing everything at one time on one day, like you did in stage one, to spreading your workouts over multiple days, working fewer body parts, with more concentration and focus.

The stage-three program will have you spending less time on each workout, but you will be adding two extra days of training per week. Instead of working your entire body just two times a week over a four-day period, like you did in stage two, in stage three, you will work your entire body twice a week, but it will be stretched over six days.

For example, on Monday you might do chest and triceps; Tuesday will be legs and calves; and Wednesday would be back, shoulders, and biceps. Thursday would be a day off, and Friday you'd begin the three-day workout cycle again. Remember to mix up the way you train those body parts and on what days you train them.

Follow these guidelines:

- Do two to four exercises per body part.
- Do three to four sets per exercise per body part (i.e., nine to twelve sets per body part).
- Rest thirty seconds between sets and one to two minutes between body parts.
- Do seven to eleven reps for upper body.
- Do fifteen to fifty reps for lower body.

Stay on the stage-three program for at least ninety days before doing any other kind of workout.

Stage Four—Senior Level

SENIOR SCHEDULE

Monday = chest
Tuesday = back
Wednesday = legs
Thursday = shoulders
Friday = triceps, biceps
Saturday = rest
Sunday = rest

Once you reach this stage of training, you will have had at least nine months of solid training behind you. With these four stages of training, you essentially have a one-year program that you can repeat year after year. I know many people who have years of great training experience who still love doing the original three-day-a-week stage-one beginner program. Once you have completed your first year of training, cycle your training workouts and keep them fresh throughout the year.

For stage four, you're going to only train your whole body once per week, but you'll do it by training only one body part each day for five days in a row and then take two days off.

For example, on Monday you would train your chest. Tuesday you would train your back. Wednesday you would train your legs and calves. Thursday you would train your shoulders. Friday you would train your triceps and biceps. Saturday and Sunday would be your days off.

Follow these guidelines:

- Do three to four exercises per body part.
- Do three to four sets per exercise per body part (i.e., nine to twelve sets per body part).
- Rest fifteen to twenty-five seconds between sets and forty-five to sixty seconds between body parts.
- Do seven to eleven reps for upper body.
- Do fifteen to 100+ reps for lower body (including higher reps for calves and quads).

Stay on the stage-four program for at least ninety days.

Mandatory Rest Breaks

One of the toughest things you'll have to do is pull yourself back from working out, especially when you're making such great progress, but it's essential that you do.

Many people keep exercising, day in, day out, year after year, with little to show for their efforts except perhaps a body that looks the same, is fast approaching burnout (especially if they've done lots of high-intensity training), and is in a rut. Far too many people find out when it is too late that if they had treated their bodies better and given themselves the rest they needed, they could have avoided being injured and maintained their motivation.

These mandatory rest breaks will help you stay injury-free and avoid the pitfalls and frustration of burnout and little or no progress. Keep your body refreshed and renewed and you will be ready, willing, and able for your next workout schedule.

When should you take some time off? I recommend *taking at least one full week off from training every four to six weeks.* That means, every month and a half, you're going to do nothing but give your body rest.

Go on "workout vacation," relax, and enjoy yourself.

You're going to find that by taking a full week off every four to six weeks your body will enjoy a state of progressive results. Week after week your body will be improving during that four-to-six-week cycle of training.

Taking a week off while your body is still in that cycle of progressive results will put you in control; you will be the one who has allowed it to stop at that higher level, and it will still be there when you come back for your next four-to-six-week cycle of training.

Think of your body as being on a continuous road upward; for each one-week period that you take off, your body will be stopping at a rest stop along the way. When you return after that week off to train again, your body will get back on the road upward to the next rest stop.

CHAPTER

STRETCHING

Don't worry, I'm not about to forget stretching. It is vitally important in each stage of training. I'm a big believer in warming up before doing any kind of exercise, especially ones with weights. Keep it simple and set aside about five to ten minutes before working out to warm up those muscles.

Some great stretches for weight training athletes are those that mimic the exercise you'll do, but with no weight. For example, if you were about to do a bench press, you might want to lie down on the bench press and perform the exercises with no weight but moving your arms up and down just in the same way you'll do the exercise holding a bar, dumbbell, or machine handles with weight.

I also like to stretch between exercises and, of course, after I've finished working a body part, such as stretching the lats after working the back, or the biceps, triceps (back of the arms), chest, quads (front of the thighs), hamstrings (back of the legs), calves. Adding stretching to your workout program will help keep you injury-free,

promote recovery and recuperation, help you feel the muscle better (remember that mind-to-muscle link), and also help give your body a more refined and sleek look.

Stretching and the Warm-Up

In the last chapter, I briefly touched on stretching before, during, and after your workout. In this chapter, I'm going to give you some stretches for specific body parts and follow with how to use cardio training to complement your stretching and warm-up.

Think of your muscles as being rubber bands. When a rubber band is cold, and you stretch it, it can easily snap. When that rubber band is warm, it's much tougher to break.

Your muscles are much the same in the sense that if you just jump right into training without warming up, those cold, unstretched muscles can easily be injured. However, give those muscles a good warm-up and the chance of that happening greatly diminishes.

And one of the great things about stretching is that it doesn't take long to do. Let's get you started by doing these basic stretches.

Chest Stretch

- Stand erect next to a vertical support bar on your machine or next to a doorway.
- Extend your arm straight out to your side and bring it up to shoulder level.
- Place the palm of that arm against the vertical support bar or doorjamb.
- Slowly turn your upper body away from that vertical support bar or doorjamb until you feel a good stretch in your chest.
- Hold it for twenty to thirty seconds, then repeat for the other side.

Biceps Stretch

- You'll still be using the same support as you did for chest and back.
- This stretch is very similar to the chest stretch, only this time the hand will not hold onto the vertical support bar or doorjamb with palm facing it but, instead, will turn the palm away from it so that the thumb is down instead of facing up.
- From there, just follow the same instructions as the chest stretch and you'll definitely feel this in the biceps.

Back Stretch

- Using that same vertical support bar or doorway, grip the bar or doorjamb with one hand and extend your arm fully out in front of you.
- With a slight bend at the knees, allow your upper body to slowly come backward until you begin feeling the lats/back stretch.

- You may then want to start turning your upper body toward your arm holding the support —as opposed to facing away from it like you did on the chest stretch—until you feel even more of a back stretch.
- Hold it for twenty to thirty seconds and repeat for the other side.

Triceps Stretch

- Raise your left arm straight up over your head.
- With your upper arm close to your head, allow the elbow to bend and the hand to come down behind and below your head.

- With your right hand, slowly pull down on your left hand or elbow. You should really feel this give the triceps a good stretch.
- Hold it for twenty to thirty seconds and repeat for the other side.

Quad Stretch

- Stand up with your body erect.
- With your right hand, grab onto a vertical support bar or doorjamb to balance yourself.
- Keeping your body erect, bend your left leg so that your foot comes behind your body.
- Keeping the upper part of the bent leg in a straight up and down line with your upper body and other leg, grab your left foot with your left hand and pull it back until your heel touches your glutes (buttocks).
- Hold it for twenty to thirty seconds and repeat for the other side.

Hamstrings Stretch

- Stand and keep your body erect.
- With only a very slight bend at the knees, bend over forward until you begin to feel the back of the legs stretching.

- As an alternative stretch, you may want to stand with both legs together and bend forward and either grab your calves/ankles or try touching the floor with your hands.
- Hold it for twenty to thirty seconds.

Calf Stretch—Feet on Floor or Elevated

- First, the feet on the floor stretch. Keep your upper body erect. Bring one leg behind you (see photo) and place your foot flat on the floor.

- The farther you bring your leg back and place your feet on the floor, the more you will feel it stretch the calf.

- Or, for the elevated version, stand on either an elevated platform that's at least six inches high or on a flight of stairs.

- Keep your body erect and place only the balls of your feet on the stairs so that your heels are not touching the stairs or platform.

- Bend only your ankles and allow your heels to come down as far as possible.

- Feel how your calves stretch just by using the weight of your body.

- You can either do one leg or both legs at a time.

- Hold the stretch for twenty to thirty seconds.

LIFE LESSON

WE'RE ONLY HERE FOR A FLICKER
I waited too long to start living.

—Anonymous

The older you get, the faster life feels like it's moving. Think back to when you were a kid. Things couldn't seem to happen fast enough. Your first date, the day you got your driver's license, graduation.

In your twenties, life seems to move a bit quicker, but there's not much time to fully realize it since so much of your time is devoted to going to college; trying different jobs and finding a career; getting into a relationship and maybe building a family; or perhaps traveling the world in search of fame, fortune, romance, and adventure. Yet, for each year that passes, the years seem like days and the hours seem like minutes.

When you were younger, people may have said to you, "Why are you in such a hurry?" "Slow down, you've got plenty of time." "You've got your whole life ahead of you." As we get older, however, we all have to pay more attention to the passing of time. How many times have you heard people say, "I'll start that new eating or exercise program soon." The truth is, soon never comes.

THE LESSON TO BE LEARNED

Each and every day you are alive is a truly precious gift. One that cannot be bought for any price. So be truly thankful for your gift of life. It was given to you for a very special reason.

Believe in yourself. Look and feel your best. Be good to yourself and start to make your dreams happen today. Dreams that inspire you. Dreams that can touch the lives of others. Dreams that will fill your life with happiness.

You can make whatever you want happen. The trap of thinking there will always be tomorrow will hold you back. One day, there won't be a tomorrow. You have no guarantee of tomorrow, and yesterday is gone and can never be recaptured. All you have is now! Yes, now is the perfect time to change your body.

Each of us has 1,440 minutes in a single day. That's 168 hours in a week and 61,320 hours in a year. If you live to the wonderful age of ninety, you will have lived a total of 32,850 days on this earth.

If you are thirty, you have already lived 10,950 of those days. If you are forty, that's 14,600 days, and if you're fifty, you've clicked off 18,250 days. I think you're catching my drift. Those days are priceless and can never be repeated or experienced again. My question to you is, what are you doing with your priceless day *today?*

CHAPTER 10

CARDIOVASCULAR/AEROBICS:

THE BIKE, STAIR STEPPER, TREADMILL, AND POWER WALK

A Few Words about the Cardio Warm-Up

To develop a body that not only looks great but feels great, you need to do some type of aerobic training. In other words, to be balanced and have all the health and appearance benefits of looking and feeling good, you need to do equal amounts of training for both the skeletal and cardiovascular systems.

The choice is yours as to when you'd like to do your cardio training and warm-up. But before I get into cardio training, let me give you a few cardio preworkout warm-up tips for training the legs.

On all aerobic training, shoot for training in your target heart range. To find this range, simply take the number 220 and subtract your age in years (for example, if you're 35, it would be 220 – 35 = 185), then take that number and keep your heart rate within 60–80 percent of it (i.e., 185 x 60% = 111 beats per minute) while you train. As with any exercise regimen, consult your doctor before setting goals.

Whether you use a bike, treadmill, or stair stepper, try to do some type of aerobic training each day or every other day. Even if it's only for a few minutes, it will at least be something to get the heart, lungs, and body moving.

You'd be surprised at how little aerobic training it actually takes to give you great results. I know you've read and heard people say that unless you're doing 30 or more minutes of aerobic training at least three times a week you're not going to get good results.

Oh yeah? I know many, many people who only do between twelve and twenty-five minutes a few days a week and have gotten incredible results, simply because they know how to do aerobic training in ways that maximize results.

I've found it beneficial to do ten to fifteen minutes of stationary bike cardio training before working legs. The pedaling motion gets the connective tissue in the knee area warmed up and also uses the legs and calves so they are ready for leg training right after the cardio warm-up.

This gives you a double benefit since you're

warming your body up and getting a nice little cardio benefit too. Just don't overexert yourself on the cardio preworkout warm-up since there could be a good chance you'll use up more energy than you may have wanted and not have as much as you need for the workout.

The great news is that it's not going to take you much time to get great results from both. You're going to have more than enough ways to get your body in shape with the weights, so don't even worry about that. Now I'm going to give you some great ways to get your cardio act together.

The Bike

The good old bike. We did it as kids, and there's no reason not to do it as adults. Whether you ride a stationary bike that sits in your garage, bedroom, den, or living room or a real one up and down the street, a bike can provide an excellent aerobic workout.

The key thing to remember about the bike is to do it long enough and fast enough to get the heart, blood, and lungs going. Lots of people will sit on a bike and peddle aimlessly and with little effort, and they never break a sweat. If you like going through the motions, then that's fine, but if you want great results, you'll need to step up the pace.

The Stair Stepper

With the stair stepper, only allow the balls of your feet to touch the steps, keeping your upper body erect and not bent forward like so many people do. Take big powerful strides up and down rather than fast, little chicken steps that only move the steps up and down a few inches. Try not to hold the rails except, if needed, to regain your balance. Keep those arms free.

The Treadmill

On the treadmill, take long strides, keeping the upper body erect and swing those arms in front and in back of you. Also, walk at a brisk pace and, after a good warm-up (three to five minutes), elevate the treadmill incline to five or more degrees and walk at that incline pace for at least ten minutes.

See, nothing complicated or fancy. Just good form making the body work more intensely. Ah, but I've saved the best for last.

The Power Walk

I had the honor of cowriting a book about the late, great Steve Reeves and doing so really opened my eyes—not only to what an incredible man he had been, but to the groundbreaking ways in which he trained.

Steve Reeves was not only Mr. America and Mr. Universe, but he was also well known for his starring roles in the *Hercules* movie of the late fifties. Reeves looked the part, and he knew how to train in ways that made him a pioneer and that are still emulated to this day.

One of the things that impressed me about Steve Reeves was the fact he was always looking for new and better ways to make exercise more effective. Those exercise refinements often led to such wonderful health benefits as increased blood flow and circulation, the strengthening of bones and connective tissue, improved heart function, increased metabolic rate and improved digestion, less stress, and more sound and restful sleep.

Reeves developed something he called the Power Walk. The only thing you need to do it is a pair of shoes. In his book *Building the Classic Physique—the Natural Way*, Reeves give loads of excellent tips—especially on how to make the Power Walk your secret weapon in whipping your body into great shape far faster than you imagined possible.

Reeves held the belief that walking was one of the best exercises you can do—a belief that was later embraced by the American Medical Association's committee on Exercise and Physical Fitness.

To Steve Reeves, what separated the Power Walk from regular walking was progressive resistance—its utilization of the principle that it's more difficult to walk quickly than slowly, to walk three miles than just one mile, to walk on an inclined grade than a flat surface, and to walk with weights than without them.

Reeves also found a wonderful benefit from this new form of walking. Even though he was in peak physical shape from all his years of weight training, he discovered that not only had power walking forcing him to breathe more deeply, but the increased circulation from the power walking

helped remove the lactic acid in his body and, as a result, he recovered much more quickly from his exercising.

The two things Reeves always made sure people understood were breathing and form. He liked doing something called "rhythmic breathing," whereby he would inhale *deeply* for three strides (right, left, right) and then exhale forcefully for three strides (left, right, left).

Reeves noted six key points that turned a regular walk into a Power Walk:

- Length of stride
- Speed of movement
- Distance traveled
- Degree of incline
- Amount of weight carried
- Rhythmic breathing

When Steve Reeves power walked, he kept his body upright, maintained a long walking stride, and moved his arms forward and backward in rhythm with his long strides. He was like a finely tuned machine, having studied the effects of movement and refined them perfectly in the creation of the Power Walk.

Reeves held that a long stride stretches the muscles in the legs, and muscles that are long look better and work better for you because they are loose. Reeves would tell people that as soon as they had perfected their stride, they should add more speed to their walk.

So, where do you begin? You could start by walking a half-mile, as Steve Reeves did, maintaining a stride and speed that's comfortable for you. Try to walk that half-mile in the eight-minute range.

When you're hitting the half-mile in eight minutes without much trouble, then add another half-mile to your distance and try to do it in thirty minutes or less.

Reeves was quite the thinker, and he found

that great results can be experienced when those who are 5-feet-6-inches or shorter go for the goal of walking that mile in fourteen minutes or less, and those who are taller than that try and make it in twelve minutes or less.

As with any exercise, resistance and intensity are key factors in determining how effective power walking can be for you. As soon as flat surfaces become too easy, then add inclined surfaces and hills. For more intensity, you can walk faster or carry some additional weight as you walk.

Reeves recommended that the beginner wanting to carry extra weight use hand weights. Of course, beginners should start with lighter weights (like one pounders) and work their way up as they become more fit. Reeves found that within a relatively short period of time, people can work up to 15 percent of their body weight in added weight.

When Reeves wanted a full power walking workout with added weight, he'd put roughly 10 percent of that weight around his waistline by wearing a weight belt and would divide the other five percent between hand and ankle weights.

The Get-in-Shape Power Walk Formula

Steve Reeves found that power walking two to three miles will get most people in shape, while walking one to two miles will keep them there.

This may not seem like much, but Reeves made the point that power walkers can burn up to 300 calories in just thirty minutes. And if they walk an hour or two a day (keeping their caloric intake the same), they can say good-bye to over one pound of fat a week. That's ten pounds in ten weeks and thirty pounds in thirty weeks. That's major.

Perhaps the biggest reason Reeves prescribed power walking was that walking is the most natural exercise there is—something people can do

their entire life without expensive equipment and with very little risk.

While power walking is good for both men and women, Reeves found that women experienced extra benefits from it. First of all, the power walk doesn't adversely impact the breasts like the constant bouncing up and down from running. It's also a great bun burner. To get this bun-burning effect, remember to use the heel-to-toe technique: the heel of the advancing foot should touch the ground first, and the knees should be kept slightly bent. As you roll to the flat foot position, straighten your leg and drive it forcefully to the rear with your buttocks muscles.

Always use the glutes as the driving force when pushing your leg to the rear, not your toes. As your front leg is driven back, the opposite leg should be thrust forward, taking as long a stride as possible.

The icing on the cake (make that low-fat) for the Power Walk is the way you swing your arms as you walk. Steve Reeves was a big believer in the benefits of swinging the arms back and forth in a pendulum-type of motion in opposition to the leg movement.

Try to bring your arms forward to an approximately forty-five-degree angle and back to approximately thirty degrees in a rhythmic fashion, so that your left arm swings forward as your right leg moves forward and your right arm swings forward as your left leg moves forward.

I want you to make power walking a part of your cardio program; it's really that good. Like any exercise, don't go overboard trying to do too much too quickly.

Start off slowly and do just a few minutes each day. Begin by power walking from wherever you park your car to school, work, or the store. Pick up the pace of your walk and notice how that feels. Build on it a little each time, and before long, you'll see and feel results.

CHAPTER 11

BODYWEIGHT-ONLY
EXERCISES

Some of the best exercises you can do are those that simply use just your body weight. I'm sure you'll remember doing some of these many years ago when you went to school. There are subtle differences in how to do them, however, and that difference can give you much better results.

Even though you're not using a barbell, dumbbells, or machines, it's still important to warm up before exercising, so don't skip that. You'll also find that simply changing the position of your body can greatly change how you feel that exercise and the results you can experience. It is important to always keep proper form in any exercise position or variation you try.

Push-Up (Chest and Triceps)

There are lots of ways to do these. The easiest is by keeping your knees touching the floor; this is much less difficult than having only your feet and hands touch the floor and keeping your knees locked and legs straight.

The further apart your hands are, the more you'll feel it in your chest. The closer the hands, the more you'll feel it in your triceps. Arms and hands in line with your upper body is much easier than arms and hands forward and in front of you. Also, elevating your legs so that they are higher than your upper body makes any variation of this exercise more difficult.

Push-Outs from Wall (Triceps and Chest)

Okay, so now you know how to do all kinds of great variations of the push-up, right? Sure you do, no problem. That's why this exercise will be a cinch to learn and even better to do.

Think of this exercise as a push-up, only standing. Keeping your body erect, stand about one to two feet away from a wall. Place your hands on the wall—use the hand-spacing tips (that tell you how to place your hands to feel it in the chest and triceps) I gave you in the push-up section—and let your upper body come forward toward the wall. Don't allow your body to bend as it comes forward; keep it straight. To increase the resistance, try placing your feet further away from the wall.

Once your upper body has come forward, push out/away so that it moves away from the wall until the arms and elbows are fully extended and locked out. Do nonstop reps and, to make it more difficult, step back even further from the wall so that your body is at a greater angle.

Pull-Up (Overhand for Back and Triceps)

The pull-up. Wow, don't you remember how tough these things were for you and just about everyone else, except for that kid who could do endless pull-ups so quickly and easily? There was always one kid in school who could do these things like it was a walk in the park.

But don't let your inability right now to do lots of pull-ups keep you from at least trying this exercise, because it's a great one. Over the years, I've known many world-champion bodybuilders who had incredible strength but couldn't do pull-ups worth a darn.

A few things to keep in mind. If you use an overhand grip, it will work your back and triceps more. Also on the overhand grip, the further apart your arms are, the more you'll feel it in the upper back and lats. The closer they are, the more you'll feel it in the middle to lower lats.

Pull-Up (Underhand for Back and Biceps)

The underhand grip will primarily hit the middle to lower lats and biceps. Many people think the biceps are worked when doing regular overhand-grip chins, but they're not really worked unless the hands are turned so the grip is underhand, just like the grip you'd use grabbing a barbell and doing a curl.

Hand distance doesn't really make that big a difference on the underhand grip as it does on the overhand grip. I've found that a roughly shoulder-width grip or perhaps a little closer feels natural.

On either overhand or underhand pull-ups, be sure to bring the upper body up as high as possible and lower it completely until the arms are fully extended.

If you have problems doing one or more reps, try putting a chair or bench just behind you and, with your knees bent, place your feet on this support to help give your body a little push as you pull your body up. Only use a little help, as it's important for you to develop your own strength on this exercise and not cheat too much.

Crunch (Middle and Upper Abs)

For this exercise, simply lie on the floor or flat bench with your legs up and kept together and your knees bent. Raise your upper body off the ground and bring it forward toward your knees. At the same time, bring your knees toward your chin.

When your body is up, it should look similar to a U or V shape. On the second rep, try to bring your upper body further forward, like you're trying to touch your knees with your upper body.

On the next rep, don't bring your upper body so far up and forward and, instead, bring your legs and knees back farther, just like you're trying to touch your chin. One rep legs back toward face, next rep upper body farther forward toward legs. Back and forth, just like that.

Throughout the exercise, do not allow your upper body to come back down and touch the floor. Keep it off the floor the whole time, since this will really keep the abs working hard. Go for higher reps in the thirty to fifty range.

Leg Lift (Lower Abs)

To do these, simply lie on the ground, platform, or flat bench. You'll want to put your hands, with palms down, under your glutes. Be sure to keep both legs together and let your legs extend out in front of you.

Keep your upper torso up and a few inches off the floor in order to keep tension on the abs. You'll then bend the knees and bring the legs up and back toward your upper body until your knees hit the ab area. Be sure to keep the feet and upper body up and off the floor from start to finish. Go for the higher reps in the twenty to fifty range.

Deep Knee Bend—Free Standing and Against Wall (Quads)

Think of doing these just like doing a squat, only with no weight. In essence, all you're really doing is keeping your upper body erect and bending the knees, squatting up and down.

Where you place your feet will affect, to some degree, where you feel the exercise. With legs close and feet pointed straight ahead you'll most likely feel it in the overall quad, and this should help give your legs a nice outer sweep.

To really make the quads burn, try doing these deep knee bends with your back against a wall. This will add resistance to the exercise, making the legs work harder, and help you maintain strict form. Try to go down to the parallel position and do nonstop, nonlockout (when the knees are bent) reps for even better results.

Feet turned out and away from the body will tend to place the emphasis on the inner thighs. Legs and feet turned farther out and away from the body—like a ballet-type stance—shift more work to the inner and upper-inner thigh. Regardless of legs and feet position, always make sure the knees travel in a straight line over the toes.

Deep Knee Bend—Free Standing and Against Wall (Quads) *(continued)*

Trunk Twist (Serratus and Side Abdominal Area) Seated or Standing

I prefer to do these with a broomstick or simply by keeping the arms up and close together and in front of the chest, sort of like a boxer would.

The key to this exercise is continuous side-to-side high reps. That's why I don't count reps, but simply minutes. Go for three to five minutes of continuous side-to-side motion for great results.

Simply take a broomstick and place it behind your neck so that it rests across your shoulders/traps, just like you'd place a barbell if you were doing a squat. Now, with lower body not moving, simply start twisting your upper body from side-to-side.

No need to twist quickly or use big sweeps of motion until after a minute or so when your body gets warmed up and loose. Then, go ahead and increase your twisting speed and range of motion. A great way to count time on this is simply to pick a favorite song—since most songs are between three to five minutes—and keep twisting until the song is finished.

Lunges—One Leg Up, One Leg Down

Stand with your body erect. Squat down, and as you do bring one leg out in front of you and let the other bend down directly in a straight line below your body with the foot behind your body.

Think of this just like you were kneeling down, only without letting your knee touch the floor and keeping the legs separated—the one that's doing the work in front of you and the non-working leg bent and below your body. High non-stop, nonlockout reps work fabulously on this exercise, so try to do fifteen to thirty reps for each leg before switching legs.

Good Mornings (Hamstrings and Lower Back)

This is a great and very simple exercise. All you have to do is stand straight up. Keep your legs and feet together. While keeping your legs straight and knees locked, bend your upper torso forward and over your feet.

Go as far forward as possible and let your upper body come down over your feet as far as possible until you really feel a good stretch in your hamstrings and lower back. Once you've reached the point where you can go no lower, bring the upper body back up and do it again. High nonstop reps of twenty to forty work well on this exercise. Be sure to breathe in on the way down and a big breath out on the way up.

Lying Upper Body Raise (Arms under Body)—Lower Back

Not much movement is needed for this exercise to really work, tone, and strengthen your lower back. Simply lie down with your stomach touching the floor. Keep your legs and feet close together. Place your arms and hands under your upper legs, with your hands turned so that your palms are touching the floor.

Slowly raise your upper body a few inches off the floor until you can feel your lower back working. Hold your body in this position for one or two seconds, and then slowly lower it back down and repeat. Be sure and do slow, continuous tension reps and you won't need to do more than five to nine per set and only two to three sets.

Walking (Aerobic)

Many say it's the best exercise for the body. You've just read about a great way to do it—the Power Walk—in Chapter 10.

Calf Raise (Calves)

This is a simple but very effective exercise for the calves, and all you have to do is bend your ankles and raise your body up and down with your feet.

Be sure to keep your body vertical with only the balls of your feet and toes on a platform or stair step. Then simply go up and down with only the ankles bending as the heels come down and go up as high and low as they can.

Lots of nonstop reps work fabulously for this exercise, lots of reps—as in more than fifty. To make it easy, forget counting reps. Just count minutes. Start off by doing two nonstop minutes of all the way up and all the way down calf raises.

You're going to feel them burn like never before and you'll want to stop when it happens, but don't. This is the point where you start making the exercise pay some big rewards.

When you can no longer do full-range reps, do partial reps. Just keep the calves moving up and down until they can no longer do both.

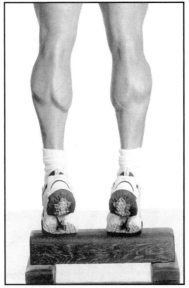

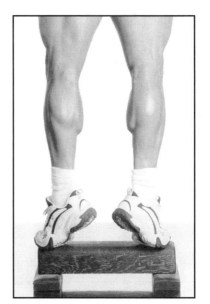

Mimicking Jumping Rope (Aerobic)

Jumping rope is one of the all-time best cardio exercises you can do. But what if you aren't very good at rope jumping, what can you do? No problem. Just jump up and down. Really. What I'd like you to do is pretend you've got a rope in your hand—you can even move your hands just like you would if you were holding a rope, but you won't have to.

Keep your body erect, with a slight bend at the knees, and start jumping up and down in place at least 100 times. Start off by jumping up only an inch or so; then, as you get used to it and that gets easy, start jumping up and down a few inches.

You can jump fast or not so fast. You can jump up just a little or you can jump higher. You can jump fifty times up and down, then rest, or jump 200 times nonstop or anything in-between—the choice is yours. And if you're looking for a great fat-burning way to start your day, do your jumping before breakfast; you'll be amazed at how something so simple can be so good for you.

CHAPTER 12

INFOMERCIAL EQUIPMENT EXERCISES

Don't even get me started about infomercials. I'm amazed that these people selling so much of this fitness stuff can sleep at night, because an ab machine is not the secret to unlocking your body's fabulous self. Not to mention that those models (genetically gifted, mind you) with the lean, tight abs used years of training, a good nutrition program, and lots of other exercises—and not that ab machine—to get those fabulous bodies.

By the way, have you ever noticed how the infomercials change every few months from legs to abs to buns to whole body to_____ . . . well, you fill in the blank. So if you bought one of those machines and it's been sitting under your bed, in your closet, down in the basement, up in the attic, or in the garage, did you waste your money? Not if you read this chapter. Follow the manufacturer's instructions for the specific equipment you are using. The following are general guidelines to help you benefit from each of those types of equipment.

If You Bought an Ab Machine

To get the most from an ab machine—the design of which is based on the crunch—work the ab exercise with short-range nonstop contractions. You don't need to go all the way up and down to work the abs effectively.

When working the abs with any crunch-type movement, the key is to making the upper body move in a semicircle where the movement sort of mimics making your upper body roll forward like it was a carpet rolling up.

That is, you're bringing your upper body up and forward in a circular motion and if possible, the legs are coming back toward the upper torso at the same time. This will really contract the abs, especially when you only allow your upper body to come back down a few inches before bringing it up again for the next rep. Continuous tension works beautifully for the abs, so keep that in mind when using whatever kind of ab machine you have.

If You Bought a Whole-Body Rider-Type Machine

This is a much better piece of infomercial equipment since it works more muscles, thereby conditioning more of the body. Basically, these machines are based around the concept of a stationary bike but have handles that move, thereby allowing you to also row and exercise your upper body at the same time.

The key to using this effectively is in the range of motion and intensity. The bigger the range of motion, the better you're able to bring more muscles into play and the harder you'll make your body work. You also get the stretching, flexibility aspect of it.

The other factor is intensity, that is, making your muscles work harder and more effectively by either working longer or doing more in less time.

If your machine has a resistance adjustment that can make it more difficult to either pedal or move those arm handles, then use it; crank it up a notch or two and feel the difference. In one workout use less resistance but pedal and row faster longer or pedal and row faster in a shorter amount of time.

In your next workout increase the intensity and work out harder, but decrease your workout time. Find the combinations of the two (and any in between) to which your body responds best.

If You Bought a Kneeling Roller–Type Machine

Many years ago, someone came up with the idea of taking a lawnmower wheel or similar kind of wheel, putting a stick or rod through the middle of it, then kneeling down with the wheel in front of them, grabbing each side of the stick and rolling the wheels forward and backward, thereby creating a fabulous abdominal, shoulder, arms, and lower back exercise.

Turn the clock up years later and now you have those beautiful celebrities who've amazingly invented a machine just like that wheel. Of course, they tell you why the lawnmower wheel doesn't work as well as their three-easy-payment machine.

If you've bought one of these, all is not lost. But write me next time before you buy one of these things and I might be able to save you some green.

Continuous tension is the key factor in getting great results from these types of machines. Start off by doing limited-range reps of only a few inches back and forth. Then, extend the range of movement and notice how you feel it.

You also want to keep the back straight and the arms in a fixed position from start –to finish. It's okay to have a slight bend to the arms or slight arch to the back, but once you've found the most comfortable positions for both, then keep them there throughout the exercise.

High nonstop reps work well too. Like any machine, these have their limitations, so find the effective exercise area for each and stay in it and you'll get great results, even from an infomercial machine.

LIFE LESSON

ALWAYS TAKE TIME TO PLAY

*You can discover more about a person in an
hour of play than in one year of conversation.*

—Plato

So many folks are so caught up in having material things, accolades, and worldly success that they've neglected a big part of their lives—play.

All work and little play makes for a very dull and boring life. You need an equal balance of work and play in order to release stress, tensions, and pent-up energies that seek expression through activities other than just work. That means taking time for yourself to exercise and do the other things you enjoy doing.

THE LESSON TO BE LEARNED

Look at some of the people society admires. Yes, a few of them do nothing but work, work, work. To them, it's their life and the only thing they know. I've known many of them—each worth hundreds of millions of dollars—and they feel like they can't stop. Like an addiction, they feel if they stop to enjoy a hobby or play, their whole world would fall apart. Talk about being chronically frustrated and deeply unhappy!

However, I've met many worth infinitely more—measured in more holistic terms—who have found that taking time to play not only fulfills that deep inner need that constantly longs to be fulfilled but also actually helps them become better in their work through the skills and discipline they learn in play. And exercise is high on their list. What a great benefit and one you can start enjoying right now!

Be active. Be vibrant. Be enthusiastic. Be like a kid again. Exercising and looking and feeling your best will help you enjoy those things you love to do even more.

CHAPTER 13

GREAT MACHINE EXERCISES

Look in any gym and you're likely to see rows of machines; even many homes are minigyms nowadays. Some are fancy and some not, but all of them are designed to make working out better and more effective.

As good as machines are, and some of them are excellent, they're still based on making the body work through a certain range of motion, in a fixed groove or track. This is where one of the biggest limitations of machine training will be found. Barbells and dumbbells don't have the kinds of limitations many machines do.

One limitation is real weight versus machine weight. Because machines have pulleys, cams, cables, and the like, much of the weight you think you're lifting has been reduced. For example, chances are that an eighty-pound dumbbell French press is going to feel different than an eighty-pound cable French press with one, two, or more pulleys that the cable travels through, which reduce resistance.

I've seen and heard stories of athletes who can power up 350 pounds on the machine bench press, only to turn blue in the face when sitting under 275 pounds with a barbell. So always keep that in mind when machine training.

Another factor to consider is whether machine training is right for your body, meaning, if you've got long arms, short arms, long legs, or short legs, then you may find that particular machines are designed to accommodate and work optimally with a different size body than yours. Another machine may work better for your body; however, you may discover, as many people do, that finding a machine that feels good for your body and works it in the fullest range of motion (if that's how you like to train) can be quite difficult.

Now, having said all that, machines do have their place in your workout program, and they can be quite effective if you're doing great machine exercises and doing them in the correct way. Here are some of the great ones I've found.

Low-Pulley Cable Curl (Biceps)

If you stand close to the low pulley, you'll find it takes a much harder pull to get the weight moving, and you'll find more movement tension.

However, if you stand away from the machine, the pull will be easier and the weight will seem lighter.

High-Pulley Cable Pressdown (Triceps)

Keep your body close to the stack of weights to make sure the cable is moving straight up and down. Pay close attention so that the cable doesn't move forward or backward at an angle. You can use a rope or a bar. The key is to make the triceps work harder, and keeping the cable moving in a tight line up and down will help ensure this.

Low-Pulley Upright Row (Traps)

The thinking here is to place your body back far enough from the low pulley in order to form a V between your body and the weight stack when you're doing the movement. Higher reps of fifteen or more work great as do descending sets.

High/Low-Pulley Cable Lateral Raise (Shoulders)

Here's a twist: Do the low pulley version of this exercise with your arm and cable behind your back rather than in front of you. For the high cable version, which works your rear deltoids, be sure to pull the cable in front of you and across your upper body.

Cable Crossover (Chest)

Many people will do these with one foot in front of them and their upper body leaning only slightly forward. Time for something different.

Try doing them with your upper body bent over at roughly a forty-five-degree angle. You should feel a better stretch.

Cable Flye (Chest)

Keep your arms and the cable in a direct line with the stack of weights. Try using an incline bench for upper chest, a flat bench for overall emphasis, and a decline bench for lower pec work.

Front and Back Pull-Down

People tell me that simply by changing grips from overhand to reverse grip, they can feel the exercise better. To feel it even more, focus on arching that back and keeping the elbows behind your body in the lowered position so you'll get a better back contraction.

High-Pulley Cable Curl (Biceps)

This might take a little getting used to, but once you do, you'll be hooked. Place a flat bench under a high pulley. Grab the high pulley bar or have someone hand it to you while lying down. Make sure your head is right underneath the high pulley. Allow your arms to come up and fully extend above your head. Lock the upper arms so they don't move. Now bend the elbows and bring the weight down toward your head with your hands. Really feel it contract your biceps. Slowly let the weight return until the arms are fully extended above your head and repeat. Do higher reps of twenty to thirty.

Low-Pulley Preacher Curl (Biceps)

It really helps if you keep your entire upper arm on the incline bench pad along with making sure the elbows are close and your hands wide. Try varying elbow and grip positions and see where you feel it most. Be sure to let the biceps stretch at the bottom (with arms extended) before curling it back up to peak contraction.

Lying Leg Curl (Hamstrings)

To feel this exercise even more, place your arms close together under your upper body so that your chest and abs actually are resting against the backs of your arms. This will help keep the rest of your body against the leg curl pad and you'll feel the hamstrings work harder.

Seated Leg Curl (Hamstrings)

High reps of twenty-plus work well for this exercise. Try leaning forward and see if those hamstrings feel this great exercise even more.

Standing Leg Curl (Hamstrings)

Keep your torso upright. Go all the way up and squeeze each rep and bring the leg all the way until you get a full stretch. Use minimal rest between sets.

Seated Calf Raise (Calves)

Think of doing this exercise with most of the weight and work being focused on the insides of your feet and over the big toes. One way to help do this is to keep the feet placed wide of the platform and turned slightly inward. Another great technique is to allow your body to come forward as you do the reps. Talk about a burn!

Leg Extension (Quads)

Be sure your body is positioned back far enough so that the area where your hamstrings and calves meet is touching the seat. Go for full extension and lock-out at the top of the exercise and a full quad stretch by having your feet come as far as possible under the seat at the bottom of the exercise. Nonstop high reps work great.

Power Rack/Smith Machine

Let's first talk about the Smith machine. This machine has two vertical guide rods whereby a barbell that's attached to them, travels up and down in a fixed groove.

The barbell only goes straight up and straight down. But even with that, some great exercises can be done on the Smith machine, such as presses, squats, shrugs, rows, and lunges. Here are a few pointers for each.

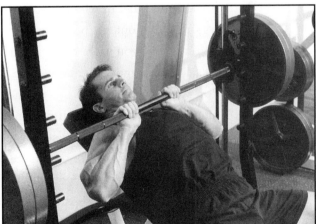

For Presses (Incline/Decline for Chest and Seated/Standing Press for Shoulders)

Keep the elbows wide and pointed away from your upper body. Keep them straight up and down and not forward or backward. Experiment with nonlockout high-rep sets and use different hand spacings to see how differently you feel it.

Lunges (Quads, Hamstrings, and Glutes)

Stand under the bar like you would if you were doing a squat. Lower the bar and, as you do, extend one leg in front of you; the other leg will bend in a straight line directly below your body with the foot behind you. Just like if you were going to kneel down, only with one leg that's doing the work in front of you. Do high reps of fifteen to thirty for each leg before switching legs.

Leg Press

Here are a few exercises and variations you can do on the leg press machine.

Vertical Leg Press (Inner Thighs/Quads/Hamstrings)

Here's an exercise that will really work wonders for those inner thighs. The key is foot position. You want to place your feet wide and turned outward on the platform. As you lower the platform, allow your legs to come out to the sides of your body and not in a straight line like you might if you were doing regular leg presses. Nonstop reps work fantastic on this movement. Be sure to get a good stretch at the bottom and don't lock your knees out at the top. Think of doing these just like a machine: up, down, up, down, no lockout and nonstop.

This is a good exercise for you to use something called strip sets. After you do five or six reps have a partner—if you have one, or you can go ahead and do it on your own—take some weight off each side; then do five or six more reps. Repeat this set and rep out until you can't do any more.

Squat (Quads)

Since the machine travels in a straight up and down line, the issue of balance becomes less of a factor, thereby allowing you to focus on new techniques. Many people use this to work inner thighs simply by changing foot position from straight forward to toes turned slightly outward. Another great one is the wide-stance squat. You'll find it beneficial if you keep your legs and feet under the bar and your knees directly over your big toes.

Row (Back)

This is a good exercise for you to use something called strip sets. After you do five or six reps have a partner—if you have one, or you can go ahead and do it on your own—take some weight off each side; then do five or six more reps. Repeat this set and rep out until you can't do any more.

CHAPTER 14

GREAT DUMBBELL EXERCISES

I think you'll find that if you'll use two to three exercises for three to four sets each per body part each training day, you'll get great results. Dumbbells are one of my favorite types of free weight training.

There's so much more freedom with range of motion, angles, and grooves that you can do with dumbbells. Not to mention, you get a better stretch. Here are some dumbbell favorites. For each exercise, always use the proper weight for your level of experience and ability.

Back: Dumbbell Row

This exercise will give you a greater range of motion and help you better work the lats. I suggest doing dumbbell rows with your opposite knee on a flat bench with your other leg slightly bent and your foot firmly on the floor.

Bring the weight down as far as comfortable in order to give your lats a great stretch. Slowly raise your elbow and raise the weight high enough so that your hand comes up right next to your chest/back. When bringing the weight down, slowly lower it until the arm holding the weight is straight and locked out and stop there. Go ahead and keep the reps in the six to ten range.

Back: Pull-Over

You'll do this exercise using a flat bench. Position your upper back against the bench. Be sure your glutes are well below the bench with only your middle and upper back coming into contact with the bench. Holding one dumbbell with both hands, keep your arms straight from start to finish.

For a great stretch, lower the dumbbell behind your body so that it's only inches above the floor. Remember to breathe like this: Take a big inhale when the weight is at the top and being lowered and a powerful, forced exhale when bringing the weight up from the bottom position. Go for fifteen to twenty reps.

Chest: Flye

With a dumbbells in each hand, lie on your back on a flat or slightly inclined bench. Raise your arms above your upper body and don't let the dumbbells touch.

Begin to lower the weights on each side, keeping them out from your body and with a slight bend at your elbows. Lower them far enough until you feel a good stretch, and then, in a semicircle (and not pressing) motion, bring the arms and weights back up to the starting position and repeat. Reps in the eight to twelve range work well.

Shoulders: Bent-Over Lateral Raise

Sitting on a bench, keep your arms slightly bent and raise the weights up and away from your body; as you do, turn your thumbs down. Reps in the twelve to fifteen range will do it.

Shoulders: Schwarzenegger Press

Sit on a bench and keep your upper torso firmly erect. Use a lifting belt if that helps. Begin the exercise with your arms to your sides and palms facing in.

Bring the weight up and as you do, turn your wrists so that your palms face forward. The elbows should be pointing out to your sides and should be kept in line with your upper torso while the weight is being lifted. You should keep them pointing downward, never back or forward, when you're lowering the weight. Go ahead and do six to twelve reps per set.

Triceps: Kickback

Start by doing some high-rep warm-up sets; then slowly add weight and decrease the reps each set. Lean forward at the waist and keep your upper arm firmly against your side.

The secret to this exercise is elbow position. Remember this: Keep the elbow higher and you'll feel it really work the triceps.

When the weight reaches the top of the movement, turn your hands so that your palms are facing upward, which will contract the triceps even harder. Do twenty reps for the warm-ups and six to ten for the heavy sets.

Triceps: Lying Extension with Dumbbells

Basically, this is the same as the lying French press done with an EZ-bar. Lie down on a flat bench, while keeping your head slightly off the end of the bench.

Take the dumbbells and as you bring the arms back, lock the arms out to about forty-five degrees. Keep the upper arms in that position and bend the elbows so that only the lower arms (forearms, wrists, and hands) move. Try using high reps in the fourteen to twenty range.

Biceps: Scott Curl

For this exercise, it's important to keep the entire upper arm against the incline pad and to slowly lower the weight until the arm is fully extended, but not hyperextended.

This can be a terrific exercise for the biceps, especially if you're wanting more fullness and emphasis on the lower biceps. Try doing both arms or one arm at a time. Curl the weight up only until you reach the point where the biceps feel the most contracted. Many people make the mistake of going past this point, thus, decreasing the effectiveness and intensity of the exercise.

A lot of people go past the point of full contraction by letting the weight come too far back, thus taking the tension off the biceps. Find the point where you feel the greatest biceps contraction; stop there and lower the weight for the next rep. Do six to nine reps with heavy weights and sixteen to twenty with lighter weights.

Biceps: Thumbs-Up Curl

This exercise will help add fullness to the biceps development. Keep the weights down at your sides with your thumbs up; then curl the weight up, keeping your thumbs in the same straight up-and-down position.

When the weights reach chest level, rotate your hands—turn the wrists up and do not allow the upper arms to move. Reps in the six to nine range work well.

Legs: Lunges

I'm sure you've seen people do lunges, but many not only do them the wrong way by using the wrong form, but they also do them with only minimal intensity, barely producing any noticeable results.

The trick is to use great form and make the quads burn by doing nonstop reps. That means no resting at the top of the exercise for a second or two before going down again. I want you doing nonstop reps, and do all the reps for the set for each leg before changing legs.

Be sure to keep your knee in a direct line over your big toe during the exercise to prevent injury. I suggest going down below parallel—the point where the upper leg is at the same horizontal angle as the floor. I think you'll feel the exercise more.

Always keep the quad of your nonworking leg in a direct line with your upper torso, not in front or behind. You can either hold the dumbbells down at your sides or up next to your shoulders, like you are doing a press (with the palms facing your face).

Legs: Stiff-Legged Deadlift

This is a truly great exercise for your hamstrings and lower back. Getting a great stretch is important to getting the most from this exercise, so if your range of motion isn't limited, you might want to stand on a wooden platform that's about four to six inches high.

Begin the exercise by holding the dumbbells to your sides. As your upper torso bends forward, rotate the dumbbells forward. Keep the weights close to your legs so that your palms will face your shins at the bottom of the exercise.

Also, keep your back slightly arched, with your head up and in line with your upper back. You can either keep your knees locked or slightly bent, depending on how you feel it.

How far down should you go? As far down as you feel that your hamstrings are fully stretched. Some people will only go down to calf level, others a little higher, and some will go as far down as the weights below their feet (if they're using a platform). Do six to eight reps per set.

GREAT BARBELL EXERCISES

Here are some great barbell exercises. A barbell is a barbell, and these exercises will work anywhere. Yes, even at home.

Always be sure to warmup. A great warm-up is doing one or two light sets of each exercise before getting into your workout. Always use great form.

Biceps: Standing Curl

Various grips will allow you to feel this exercise differently. Try an underhand grip slightly wider than shoulder-width and keep your elbows locked to your sides. Bring the weight up until you feel your biceps fully contracted. On another set, use a closer grip to hit the outer biceps and a wider grip to hit the inner biceps. Keep the reps in the five to nine range.

Biceps: Reverse Curl

Very similar to the standing barbell curl, only you'll be using an overhand grip instead of an underhand grip. Again, keep the elbows close to the sides. Use nonstop reps, increasing them to more than eighteen.

Chest: Bench Press

Lie down on a flat bench and take a grip slightly wider than shoulder-width on the barbell. You might find more power if you keep your elbows close to your sides while doing this exercise (a little secret of the big power bench pressers).

Inhale deeply as you lower the weight. As you bring the weight back up, blow that deep breath out and do it all again for the next rep.

If you want to feel the exercise work more of your upper chest, bring the bar to the neck and your elbows back to shoulder level. Reps in the eight to ten rep range per set should give you excellent results.

Chest: Close-Grip Bench Press

You'll be using the same form as the flat bench, only this time your hands will be spaced about six to eight inches apart. Try using higher reps, in the twelve to eighteen range.

Chest: Incline Barbell Press

Another exercise that's similar to the flat bench press only you're going to use an incline bench that will direct the work to the upper chest. Experiment by moving your hands and grip to see how you feel it in different areas of your chest (i.e., hands close for more inner, hands wide for more outer chest focus). Let's keep the reps in the eight to twelve range.

Shoulders: Overhead Press

Lots of options here. You can do them standing, seated, in front of the neck, or behind the neck.

Whichever you choose, use an overhand grip slightly wider than shoulder-width, and lower the bar behind your neck to the upper traps (or the upper-clavicle area if you prefer pressing from the front) and keep the elbows pointed down and not back. Nonstop reps will really make the delts burn so do no fewer than eight and as many as twelve or more, if possible.

Trapezoids: Upright Row

Go ahead and use a shoulder-width overhand grip. Remember to keep the bar close to your body and raise it up to about chin level but not much higher.

Try these hand spacings: close hands hit more traps; wide hands hit more delts. Go for eleven or more reps.

Trapezoids: Shrug

Here's a couple of ways to do a great exercise for your traps. In front of your body, use a shoulder-width grip and keep your arms locked and shrug your shoulders straight up (don't roll them) toward your ears.

Behind your body, use an overhand grip with your palms facing away from you. Keep the arms straight and shrug the shoulders straight up and down. Keep the reps in the seven to ten range.

Back: Deadlift

One of the exercises you can do for lower back, traps, glutes, and legs. Depending on your grip strength you can either use an over/underhand grip (one hand over, the other under) or the double overhand grip. Stay away from double underhand grips.

Place your feet at about shoulder-width. Keep the arms fully extended. Allow your body to squat down until the upper legs are about parallel to the floor. Keep the back locked in position and your head up. The chest will be positioned slightly forward and over the bar.

Now that your body is in the locked position, bring the legs up and lock them out, thereby raising the weight up. As the legs begin to lock out, let the upper body come up until it is straight up and down and in line with the legs. I've found reps in the five to seven range work well for this exercise.

Back: Bent-Over Row

You have two choices here: overhand and underhand grip. For the overhand grip, keep your legs slightly bent, lean forward at the waist and take a grip slightly wider than shoulder-width; then bring the weight up into your midsection and your arms back.

For the underhand grip, keep the legs slightly bent and the upper body leaning forward. Lower the weight until the arms reach full extension. As you pull the weight back, feel the back muscles contracting. It will help if you pull your arms back and the weight into your waist. A great rep range is six to nine.

Hamstrings: Stiff-Legged Deadlift

A very effective exercise that's similar to the regular deadlift but with a key difference: these will be done on a platform for a greater stretch, and the legs should remain in a nearly locked-out position (knees slightly bent) from start to finish.

Let's begin by first going as far down as you comfortably can. Do not round your back as you do these, as that only takes away from the effectiveness of the exercise. Keep the back slightly arched. Keep the reps in the five to seven range.

Quadriceps: Squat

Hey, I won't sugarcoat things. Squats can be tough, but they are great leg exercise indeed. If you're doing back squats, let the bar rest high on your upper-back/shoulder area, somewhere on the traps. Place the feet about shoulder-width apart and turn them slightly out.

With a slight arch in your lower back and your head up and looking straight ahead, squat down until your thighs are about parallel to the floor. You always want to make sure your knees travel in a direct line over your big toes. Think: Keep the knees moving/working in a straight line for more stability. You may want to slightly elevate your heels. Eight to twelve reps should do the trick.

Quadriceps: Hack Squat

The real secret to making this exercise work is to hold the barbell tightly pressed against your glutes from start to finish.

Your heels should be elevated slightly and your upper body erect. Place the bar against your lower glutes where they join the upper hamstrings or back of the legs. Squat down until your thighs are about parallel to the floor. Come back up but don't lock out. The focus is to keep constant tension on the quads. Keep the legs about eight to ten inches apart and your feet pointed straight. Nonstop reps work fabulously on this exercise, and, believe me, you'll feel the burn. Try thirteen to seventeen reps.

Inner Thighs: Wide-Stance Squats

Essentially, you'll be using the same upper body position as the regular squat, only for this one, you'll keep the legs and feet about two to three feet apart, and you'll be turning the feet out-ward (always making sure the knees travel in line over the big toes), which will focus the exercise on working the inner thighs. A higher number of reps work well, twelve to sixteen.

Forearms: Wrist Curl

Most people don't even think about doing specific exercises for the forearms; however, if you'd like a little extra gripping power, then try this. Place the arms on a flat bench and keep your wrists (with the palms up) just slightly over the edge of the bench.

Here's the biggy: keep your arms resting on the flat bench and don't let them lift up. Let the wrists relax, then bring your hands up as you curl the weight toward your forearms. You'll find that the forearms respond surprisingly well to nonstop high reps (full and partial reps, too). Let's not count reps and just go for the burn.

Forearms: Reverse Wrist Curl

This is an easy one, since it's essentially the same movement as the wrist curl, only with an overhand grip. Again there is no need to count reps, just go for the burn.

LIFE LESSON

INSIDE OF YOU IS A VOICE THAT IS ALWAYS CALLING YOU TO CHANGE

Be content with what you have; never with what you are.

—B. C. Forbe Emerson

Just when you've achieved that great-looking body, or anything else you've wanted in your life, there it is—that voice from within. Gee, I mean here you are, you've worked your tail off to get here and no sooner than you arrive, there's that voice again, telling you to enjoy your success but not to get too comfortable, because soon it'll be time to change.

Face it; you resist change because you're comfortable. It took you a while to arrive where you are, and life feels good to you now. Yet inside each of us there is a voice telling us, "Enjoy your success, but you can only stay here for a short time. Then it's time to move on and grow if you really want to be the great success you're designed to be."

Most people fear change. They want to know the end result before they make any decision, yet life doesn't work that way. So to avoid change, the majority of people have found a way to take their minds off of their own lives—often by getting caught up in other people's lives.

Look around you. How many people do you know, hear of, or see who are so busy getting caught up in what's going on in other people's lives, living in the past, or reacting to the events that life presents to them that their minds are never on their own lives and what would truly give them deep fulfillment and happiness? I bet it is a lot!

Makes you wonder why so many great people have settled for so little when they can have so much? Why have they let their major purpose in life be to worry about the lives of others or to just get through the day by ignoring their problems? These people tend to live by the creed of "maximum worry for minimum results." No wonder they're constantly frustrated and unhappy.

Know this: The desire for change—physical and otherwise—is always knocking at your door. The question is: Do you believe enough in yourself and your dreams to make life pay off on your terms? Are you one of those rare people who are living the kind of life that makes you happiest? If not, why are you afraid of change? The answer will seem silly.

THE LESSON TO BE LEARNED

Embrace the desire inside of you to change, to grow, to learn, to experience, and to be all that you were meant to be. Change is good—very good. Because the law of nature is either you grow or you die—there's no in-between.

If you have the desire for change—to change your body and life—that means only one thing: you are alive! Embrace your gift of life, for truly you are someone who was meant to be uniquely spectacular. Living a life of positive constant change will help you become that which you were meant to be.

BANISH THE FUTURE; LIVE ONLY FOR THE HOUR AND ITS ALLOTTED WORK. THINK NOT OF THE AMOUNT OF WORK TO BE ACCOMPLISHED, THE DIFFICULTIES TO BE OVERCOME, BUT SET EARNESTLY AT THE LITTLE TASK AT YOUR ELBOW, LETTING THAT BE SUFFICIENT FOR THE DAY.

—OSLER

Part IV: Body Specific

CHAPTER 16

THE DELTOIDS (SHOULDERS)

Let's get into some great exercises you can do at home. In this chapter, we'll talk about exercises for the front, side, and rear delts, in order to give you a well-balanced look.

Standing/Seated Dumbbell Side Laterals

The choice is yours here. The upper body will do the same thing for both exercises. The only thing that changes is the lower body, so you can either sit or stand.

Either way, you want your upper body to be vertically erect, straight up and down. Your arms will be fully extended and the dumbbells will be held close to your sides when you start the exercise. You'll then raise both arms up and away from your body at the sides.

Once the dumbbells and arms reach shoulder level, stop; then slowly lower them back down again and repeat. Many people find that if their arms go higher than shoulder level, they start feeling it more in the traps and less in the delts.

The delts respond very well to nonstop high reps, so keep that in mind when working them. Some people will turn their wrists slightly forward (with the thumbs pointing toward the floor) once they reach the top of the exercise. Others say they don't feel any difference doing it like that; see which way feels best for you.

Bent-Over Dumbbell Laterals

This is a great exercise to hit the rear head of the deltoid (the one located closest to your back). You can also do these standing or seated. The only difference will be the upper body position. Instead of keeping the upper body upright and erect, you'll bend forward until your head is over your feet and the upper torso is about parallel to the floor.

Nonstop reps work great on all deltoid exercises and this one is no exception. Don't allow the weights to stop at either the top or starting position. Keep them moving!

Dumbbell Pendulum-Style Side Laterals

Not many people know about this one. Before using any weights, I want you to practice the movement. Be sure your upper body is erect with both arms being down at your sides. Begin by raising the left arm out to the side up to about level with your shoulder.

Allow the left arm to come back down and, as you do, raise the right arm to the same shoulder height you did on the left arm. I think of this exercise as being performed in a pendulum-style with the left arm up and the right arm down, the right arm up and the left arm down.

Don't worry if you can't use heavy weights for this; you won't need them. This is not a power exercise, and its key importance is on form; slow, continuous rep burning; and making the delts work harder and in ways they're not used to. Stay in the fourteen to twenty-two rep range.

Dumbbell Partial Side Laterals

For this one, you'll need to use a weight that's at least twice as heavy as you'd normally use for regular side laterals. Keep your arms locked and hold the weight out to your side; then raise the weight out to your sides and away from your body.

Don't count reps. I want you do as many as possible. In fact, keep moving the weight until you can't do it any longer. Remember, nonstop reps work best. The trick is in keeping the weight moving up and down, even if its only a few inches at a time. What a burn!

Standing One-Arm Dumbbell Press

Very similar in movement to the regular two-arm dumbbell press. Simply use a weight you can press for nine to twelve reps and stand erect, holding onto a vertical bar or top of an incline bench with your other hand for upper body support and stabilization.

Begin the exercise by lowering the weight to shoulder-level, and then, keeping the upper torso upright, press the weight up until it is directly overhead and your arm is locked. Do nine to twelve reps for that arm before switching hands and working the other side.

Wide-Grip Upright Row

Did you know that simply by changing grip on that old trap favorite, the barbell upright row, you can turn it into a great deltoid exercise too? Just remember: wide grip works side delts. Try different grip spacings to zero in on where your hands need to be to feel it in the delts best. Keep the elbows high as you pull up the weight and go for eleven to thirteen reps.

Incline Bench Lateral

This exercise will work the rear deltoid, and you'll have to try a few sets and reps in order to find the right groove (where you feel it best) for you. If possible, use an incline bench and adjust it between twenty and forty degrees.

Lie on your side against the bench pad. With your outside hand, grab the dumbbell and extend your arm nearly straight down in front of you. Raise your arm out to your side as if you're doing a lateral raise, trying to keep the same angle in your elbow at all times. Raise your arm until it's directly above your upper torso.

At the top of the movement, turn your wrist so that your little finger is higher than your thumb. Slowly lower the weight to keep tension on the delt you're working. Do fifteen to twenty-five reps before working the other side.

Reverse Pec Deck

Chances are, if you've got a home gym machine setup, you'll be able to do the pec dec (facing forward) for your chest and the reverse pec dec (facing toward the back pad) for your deltoids. Two great exercises from just one machine!

I like to think of my hands as hooks as they hold the pec dec pads/bars. But don't grip too tightly or you'll feel it too much in your wrists and forearms. Position your upper body upright on the seat with a slight arch in your lower back and away from the back pad and your chest close to the back pad. It will help if you keep your elbows up and your arms in a locked range of motion by not changing the angle of bend in the elbows.

Pull the handles and your elbows as far back as you can. You might even try raising your elbows as you do this exercise as it may add more intensity to the exercise. Go for twenty to twenty-five reps.

One-Arm Alternate Front Raise—Dumbbell/Cable

An ideal exercise for the front delts. Keep doing those non-stop continuous reps because they work great. When using dumbbells and cables remember this sequence: one arm comes down and the other arm goes up.

Let's change a few things by raising the weights higher than your shoulders, as compared to side laterals where I only wanted you to raise to shoulder level. If you're looking for an even greater contraction, bring the weights directly overhead. Target the reps in the twelve to sixteen range per side.

Front of Body/Behind-Back Lateral Cable Raise

If your home gym has a low cable pulley attachment (many of them do), then give this a try. You'll need to stand next to a lower cable and have the delt you are working positioned farthest away from the weight stack.

You can either do these with the cable in front of your body (see picture) or with the cable behind the body. Reach behind your back for the handle. While keeping your upper body erect, raise your arm until it's above shoulder level. Keep your elbow in the same position from start to finish. Slowly lower the arm only as far down as you can still feel some tension on the delt.

Remember, nonstop reps and constant tension. Try twelve to eighteen reps for each side.

Front Barbell Raise

Much like the dumbbell and cable front raise you just read about, but this time with a barbell and you'll be working both delts at the same time. Forget the heavy weights on this.

For a change of pace, use different widths of grip to see how they hit those front delts. Try narrow, medium, and wide grips and see which one causes you to feel it more. Once you find the best one for you, stay with it until it stops giving you great results; then experiment again and find the new grip width that does. Do twelve to sixteen reps.

CHAPTER 17

THE CHEST

While many people will train the chest, far too many of them aren't doing it as effectively as they could. Let's change that for you.

Time after time, the solid basic movements work best. Yes, there are lots of machines to work the chest, but you still can't beat the results you'll get by using good old barbells and dumbbells. The great thing is, you can do these at home. Put these on your "must try" list.

Incline Barbell Press

I prefer these above any other bench press. A few things to remember to make these work for you. First, keep your body tight in the seat, and don't let your glutes come up. Next, find what hand spacing feels most comfortable. Perhaps it's shoulder-width? Maybe it's slightly narrower or wider? For each grip used, bring the elbows down and back and make the bar touch the top of your upper pec, just below the neck.

Keep the reps in the eight to twelve range.

Incline Dumbbell Press

I told you how much I like incline presses. As far as chest exercises go, this would have to be my all-time favorite. Dumbbells help you get a fuller range of motion by giving you a deeper stretch than a barbell can. I also like dumbbells because the exercise groove isn't as fixed as it is when you use a barbell or machine. The hidden benefit of using dumbbells is in working muscles that act as stabi-lizers (delts, triceps), which are needed for overall tone, strength, development, and injury prevention.

You're only as strong or as well balanced as your weakest link (such as those muscles that act as stabilizers), so focus on exercises, like dumbbells, that use them and you'll get lots of benefits from your training. I like the same rep range as barbell inclines—eight to twelve.

Bench Press—Barbell and Dumbbell

Well, I can't really give you great exercises for the chest unless I include this one. As much as I prefer inclines over the flat bench, many people have built great chests from this exercise. Here are a few tips to help you get the most from it. The arms should be close to the body as you lower and press up the weight.

Breathe like this: deep breath in as you lower the weight and big breath out as you press the weight up.

Keep your feet flat on the ground and your upper body and glutes on the bench—none of this "arching the back off the bench just to get the weight up" stuff. If that's happening, you're using too much weight or your form is wrong.

Reps in the six to ten range work well.

Dumbbell Flye

Many people like this exercise as a shaping movement for the chest. However, you can also use this as a main chest exercise. Choose either a flat or incline bench. Incline tends to work more upper chest.

Think of doing this like hugging a barrel. As you press the weight up, the arm motion should be wide and arching, similar to putting your arms around a big tree. Allow the elbows to be bent slightly and the arms wide, and to keep tension on the chest at the top of the movement, don't let the dumbbells touch each other. Keep them about five to eight inches apart when your arms come above your body.

Do higher reps of nine to fourteen.

Dips

If you have access to a dip bar(s), then you really should give this exercise a go. Dips happen to be one of the best lower-pec mass builders out there. Be sure to really warm up well before doing dips, especially the elbows. I'd put this exercise as the second or third exercise in your chest workout, just to make sure the chest and elbows are thoroughly warmed up.

You want to keep your upper body fairly upright and your arms close to your sides from start to finish. You can either keep the legs hanging straight up and down or bend the knees so that your feet are up and behind you.

Bend the elbows and lower your body as far down as possible, and then press your body up until the arms are fully locked out.

Begin with as many reps as you can do and shoot for more then ten if possible. If you're doing more than fifteen reps with your bodyweight, try using a dipping belt, whereby you can add a dumbbell to your bodyweight for more resistance.

After the warm-up set, do eight to fifteen reps per set.

Vertical Pec Press

Some home machines will have this feature, and it can be a great one if you do it right. Actually, it's quite similar to a machine bench press where you're lying down. The biggest difference is that you'll be keeping your upper body vertical and against the back pad.

Keep your arms close to your upper body. To hit more inner chest, move your hands in closer together. For outer chest emphasis, move the hands out farther away from each other.

Do fourteen to twenty reps.

Close-Hand Push-Up

Push-ups are one of the best chest and triceps exercises anyone can do at home. However, did you know that simply changing your body angle will let you work the chest in different ways? Here's how: I suggest that you find a flat bench or chair that's at least fifteen inches high. Put your feet up on the bench instead of on the floor. Your hands and the front of your upper body will rest on the floor.

Place your hands—one on top of the other—under your lower chest. Keep your entire body perfectly rigid, and then press your body off the floor until your elbows are locked out. Lower your body back down to the floor again and repeat.

Do ten reps to start. After the warm-up set, do eight to fifteen reps per set. If you're able to do fifteen or more reps easily, then try raising your feet even higher above the rest of your body.

LIFE LESSON

IF THOUGHTS CAN HURT YOU, THEY CAN ALSO HEAL YOU

Worry affects the circulation—the heart, the glands, the whole nervous system. I have never known anyone who died from overwork, but many who died from doubt.

—Dr. Charles Mayo

The power of your thoughts. Few people think about it. Even fewer understand just how powerful they are. Your thoughts have incredible power to improve your body and your life—or destroy it. You're the one who decides which it will be.

As you've learned, the thoughts you think create the realities you experience. Your thoughts are like powerful magnets that attract into your life those things that are in perfect harmony with the type of thoughts you think.

Negative thoughts attract negative people and experiences. Positive thoughts attract positive people and fulfilling, happy experiences. Your family and friends don't have any influence over the thoughts you choose to think. You're the only one.

THE LESSON TO BE LEARNED

To show you how powerful your thoughts are: many diseases and sickness—some of them caused from lack of exercise and poor nutrition—are the result of one's thinking.

You've no doubt heard what fear and worry can do to the mind and the body. Now I want you to consider the power of choice—making the choices that you do and the outcome from those choices. Here's just one example.

Many people smoke. And it's by the nature of their thoughts that they've chosen to smoke. They know the dangers. Still, they chose to smoke. They could quit at any time if they deeply desired to. But they keep on smoking until one day it's too late. Their lives are now measured in breaths and not days, months, or years.

Their thinking killed them. Smoking was only one of the many ways they did it to themselves. There weren't any victims, only willing participants.

It sounds cold doesn't it? The reality is, we've all probably known someone very dear to us whose life ended way too soon for a reason that could've been prevented—if only that person's thoughts had been directed in a different direction: positive, healthful, worry-free and fear-free.

Right now, you have that same choice. Will your thoughts be life giving or life taking? Build your body, your mind, and your spirit and say yes to life, for life is always saying yes to you.

CHAPTER 18

THE BICEPS

People love looking at arms that are well toned and in shape. When someone wants to know if you're working out, doesn't he or she typically squeeze your arm? Well, if your arms are less than what you want them to be, never fear, help is here. We'll start with the biceps and some exercises with different twists.

Lying Dumbbell Curl

People are amazed at how much they feel this exercise stretch, peak contract, and work the biceps. The key is elbow position. You want the elbows to be tucked close into the bench and to remain there during the exercise. The arms should be held out and away from the body, and the hands should be almost as far back as the delts.

When your arms are in this position, the curling action is already in a great place where you'll really feel the exercise work. Forget about heavy weights. First of all, this disadvantaged lever position won't allow you to handle anything heavy, which is fine.

Simply choose a moderate weight (probably 30 to 60 percent of your regular eight-rep curling weight) and go for thirteen to nineteen nonstop reps with both arms at the same time.

Barbell Concentration Curl Bending Down

I'd like you to use a close grip on the barbell. No need to go heavy on this one either, since the focus of the exercise will be on using higher reps and getting a peak contraction.

Squat down and place your arms against the inside or on top of your thighs. Keep your upper torso erect. Curl the barbell up to chin level and hold the peak contraction for one or two seconds, then slowly lower the weight until the arms are again fully extended.

Go for twenty to thirty reps.

Kneeling Cable Curl

Sit or kneel down in front of the low pulley attached to your machine's weight stack. Grab hold of either a curved or straight bar that will be attached to this low-pulley cable.

Let your arms extend before beginning the exercise and, with your elbows into your sides, curl the weight up and back toward you. Stop when you feel a full contraction in your biceps. Lower the bar back to the starting position.

Do sixteen to twenty-two reps.

Thumbs-Up Curl

These are great for building the biceps. The important thing will be your hand position.

Begin with your arms close to your body and curl the weight (dumbbells) up with your palms facing the ceiling. Bring the weight to about shoulder level or until you feel a peak contraction in the biceps.

At the top of the exercise, turn your palms down and keep them in this position until the arms are fully extended. On the way down, turn your hands so the weights will be lowered out and away from your body.

Do eight to eleven reps.

Barbell Curl with Back Against Wall—Vertical Support

A lot of people cheat when they do regular barbell curls simply by using too much back or leg motion to help curl the weight up. You can't do that with this exercise.

With a lighter barbell than you'd normally use for a regular barbell curl, place your upper body, from the glutes to the head, against a wall. You'll keep your upper body there from start to finish.

Be sure that your upper arms and elbows are close to your sides. With the weight hanging down and your arms fully extended, curl the weight up until the biceps are peak contracted. Slowly lower the weight back down and repeat.

Do twelve to fifteen reps.

CHAPTER 19

THE TRICEPS

To get the most from your triceps exercises, you need to pay close attention to how you place your upper arm and elbow. The further away they are from your upper body, the less weight you'll be able to use and the less you'll feel the exercise.

You also need to make sure your triceps are thoroughly warmed up before working them with moderate to heavy weights. The triceps tendon and elbow joint are not among the strongest joints and tendons in the body, so to make them stronger, take a little extra warm-up time (just a few light weight sets should do it).

Bench Press Using Close-Grip

Do these the same way you'd do a flat bench press with the only difference being where your hands grip the barbell. Just changing your hand spacing will give you a fabulous exercise for the backs of your arms. They should be at least five to nine inches apart. Keep your arms close to your body throughout the exercise.

Lower the bar until your hands touch your chest; then press it back up until your elbows are completely locked out and the weight is directly over your face. Elbow lock-out means triceps contraction, and that's what you want on these.

Do five to nine reps.

Cable French Press

You can do this exercise either standing, seated, kneeling, or lying on your back. The relative upper body position is what will be ultimately important here. This exercise will really work the outer long muscle of the triceps. Remember to keep your upper arms close to your head from start to finish.

Grab the bar or rope that connects to the low pulley on your machine. Bring your hands as far down behind you as possible in order to give the triceps a great stretch. Raise the bar or rope above you until your arms are fully extended and elbows are locked. Lower the arms back down.

Do higher reps in the twenty to thirty range.

Dumbbell French Press Using One or Two Hands

These are like squats for the back of the arms, especially when you get up into the heavy weights. Make this exercise the second or third one after making sure your triceps tendon and elbow areas were warmed up from a previous triceps exercise.

Go slowly if you're looking to increase the weight you use for each set. This is a tough but great exercise for the triceps, so take a little extra time doing it right.

Use higher rep/lighter weight sets and go progressively heavier with fewer reps as you do more sets. You can do these standing or seated. Be sure to keep your upper torso upright.

Bring the dumbbell over your head. Let the dumbbell come down as far as comfortably possible behind your head and then bring your arm back up until the elbow(s) is fully locked out.

Do twelve to twenty reps.

Bench/Chair Dip

I've found this to be a super exercise for adding size and shape to the lower triceps, the area above the elbow. You'll need to use a flat bench to place your hands on and either another bench or a chair that's about three to four feet away from you, to place your heels on.

Think of this position as being like a body bridge, with your feet put in front of you and your hands/arms holding your body up off the ground.

You want your upper arms close to your body and your elbows pointing behind you. Bend your elbows and let your body come down as far as possible, and then straighten your arms and bring the body back up.

Do as many nonstop continuous reps as you can with your goal being fifteen to twenty reps. If you can do fifteen to twenty reps, and they were easy, then try putting a weight plate on top of your lap to give your body a little extra weight.

Overhead Extension Using Rope or Bar

Bend over and lean forward. Now extend your arms over your head. Congratulations, you've just worked the long head of the triceps. Easy as can be, and now you can step it up and really work your triceps.

Attach a bar or rope to a cable on the high pulley of your machine. Turn away from the machine. Now, lean your upper body forward and bend over at the waist.

Bring the upper arms close to your head and keep them in this position from start to finish. Extend your arms as you bring the bar or rope out in front of you. Lock those elbows out and really make the triceps work.

You can also do this exercise with one arm at a time simply by using a stirrup-style handle. Go for reps in the sixteen to twenty-four range.

One-Arm Press-Down with Reverse Grip

The regular two-arm press-down is easy: Keeping your arms close to your upper body and your hands about twelve to sixteen inches apart, press the weight down until the elbows are locked out, then allow the weight to come back up until it reaches the lower chest level and repeat.

Now it's time to do the press-down with an underhand grip—also called a reverse grip. Use a stirrup handle and one arm at a time. Do these just like the regular press-down. The only difference is you'll be using one hand at a time instead of two.

Do fifteen to twenty-five reps.

Two-Arm Barbell Kickback

You've probably seen dumbbell kickbacks. You know, when the person doing them bends the upper body forward and keeps his working arm to his side, then, with a dumbbell in his hand, brings the weight back (a sort of kickback-type action) behind his body until the elbow is locked out.

This exercise is similar to that since you will be extending the arms back behind you, but this time, you won't be using a dumbbell, you'll be using a lighter barbell.

Place a barbell on the ground; then turn around, squat down, and pick it up so that your palms are facing behind you.

Hold the barbell behind you, bend over forward and keep your arms close to your body. Bring the arms and weight behind you by extending your arms and locking out your elbows. Try to hold the barbell in this position for a second or so; then, while keeping your arms close to your body, bend the elbows and allow the weight to return to the starting position.

Go for as many reps as you can do.

CHAPTER

THE ABS

With so many different abdominal exercises you can do, which do you choose? If you're like many who work out at home, you may not have access to all the different kinds of ab machines, but you're simply looking for a few great ab exercises that are simple and very effective.

Let's focus on three ab regions: upper, lower, and sides. Crunches typically hit the upper/middle abs. Knee-ups will work lower abs, and trunk twists will work the side abdominal region.

When working the abs, it is important that you do nonstop reps and only take a minimal (not more than twenty-five seconds) rest between sets. Also keep in mind the benefits of short-range movements. The abs can be worked with incredible intensity and effectiveness when constant tension is placed on them from doing nonstop short-range reps. In many exercises, just a few inches of movement is all it takes.

Crunch

Simply lie on the floor or flat bench and bring your legs up with your knees bent and legs together. Bring your upper body up and off the ground and let it go forward toward your knees. At the same time, bring your legs up and back toward your chin.

When your body is up, it should look similar to a U shape. On the second rep, try to bring your upper body farther forward, like you're trying to touch your knees with your upper body.

On the next rep, don't bring your upper body so far up and forward; instead, bring your legs and knees back farther, as if you're trying to touch your chin. One rep, legs back toward face; next rep, upper body farther forward toward legs. Back and forth, just like that.

Throughout the exercise, do not allow your upper body to come back down and touch the floor. Keep it off the floor the whole time, since this will really keep the abs working hard.

Go for higher reps in the thirty to fifty range.

Crunch with Legs Moving

Think of how you just did that last crunch, and the big difference on this one will be that your legs will be moving back and forth, just as if you are doing circles or pedaling a bike.

Again, do nonstop short-range reps; keep the upper body up and off the floor and really bring the upper body up and forward toward your knees.

High reps in the twenty-five to fifty range work well on this.

Knee-Ups (Hanging or Lying)

There are two great ways to do these. If you have a pull-up bar that will allow you to hang from it, use it by simply keeping the arms straight and body up and down and bring only the knees and legs up and back toward your stomach. The upper body should only bend/curve slightly as the knees come up and back into your stomach area.

The other way to do these is simply by lying on the ground, a platform, or flat bench. You'll want to put your hands, with palms down, under your glutes. Be sure to keep both legs together and let your legs extend out in front of you.

Keep your upper torso up and a few inches off the floor in order to keep tension on the abs. You'll then bend the knees and bring the legs up and back toward your upper body until your knees hit the ab area. Be sure to keep the feet and upper body up and off the floor from start to finish.

Go for the higher reps in the twenty-five to fifty range.

Knee-Ups (Hanging or Lying) *(continued)*

Seated or Standing Trunk Twist

I prefer to do these with a broomstick, but you can use simply no weight at all. Not that a broomstick weighs much, mind you.

The key to this exercise is continuous side-to-side high reps—which is why I don't count reps, but simply minutes. Go for three to five minutes' continuous side-to-side motion for great results.

Take a broomstick and place it behind your neck so that it rests across your shoulders/traps, just like you'd place a barbell if you were doing a squat. Now, with lower body not moving, simply start twisting your upper body from side to side.

There's no need to twist quickly or use big sweeps of motion until after a minute or so when your body gets warmed up and loose. Then, go ahead and increase your twisting speed and range of motion. A great way to count time on this is simply pick a favorite song—since most songs are between three to five minutes—and start twisting and keep twisting until the song is finished.

LIFE LESSON

EXPECT ONLY THE VERY BEST

It's a funny thing about life; if you refuse to accept anything but the best, you very often get it.

—W. Somerset Maugham

One of the biggest disappointments in life is unfulfilled expectations. Think about it: How many times in the past have you been disappointed when that new workout, piece of equipment, or diet didn't give you the kinds of results you had expected? It is rare when things in our lives exceed our expectations, but when they do, it's marvelous.

THE LESSON TO BE LEARNED

Forget about expecting anything to happen in exactly the way you think it should. People and life don't work that way. And who says your way is the best way anyhow, just because you may think it is?

The most enjoyable course to take is just to experience the moment. Enjoy each new experience that comes your way as something entirely unique and special. All new experiences are able to bring much depth, learning, and meaning to your life.

Focus your mind on only expecting the best, without so narrowly defining what "the best" must be. Stop putting labels on people, places, experiences, and events. Do the best you can and let life bring to you what you need at that particular time in your life. You can absolutely trust that it will be the right thing, too. Just expect that things will always turn out the very best way and you will get the best, every day and in every way for your life.

CHAPTER 21

THE QUADS

Why is it that so many people will train their upper bodies like crazy, but seem to completely forget about their legs? And they look like it!

You don't need some fancy leg machine that costs thousands of dollars to turn those ordinary legs into something extraordinary. Really. All you need are a few great leg and calf (hamstring and quads) exercises and the know-how to do them right.

Here are some excellent ones for your quads.

Leg Extension

This is a good exercise to warm up the knee area and quads. High nonstop reps work great on leg extensions. The big thing to remember is feeling the quads work as you do this. Some people will use full range of motion and do continuous reps.

Others will use a combination of full range reps and then partial reps. The partial rep only allows the feet to come down a few inches before

extending the legs again, locking the legs out, and squeezing the quads for one or two seconds before doing the next rep.

You might want to try doing a set with your feet pointed forward, another set with your feet turned and pointed toward each other, and a third set with feet turned outward. Many people swear by this, saying they feel it in different areas of the quad.

Go for reps in the fifteen to twenty-five range.

Hack Squat

Okay, after leg extensions, your quads should be warmed up and ready for this incredible leg exercise. Since you probably won't have access to a hack squat machine, I'm going to have you do these with a barbell. You can also do them with a dumbbell if you prefer. It's just that they are a little tougher to do with a dumbbell than a barbell.

To help with balance, you'll want to elevate your heels. I suggest using a one- to two-inch block of wood or two twenty-five-pound barbell plates. You'll then bend down and grab a barbell so that you are holding it behind you. The barbell should be held high and tight against the bottom of your glutes.

Place your feet seven to eleven inches apart, and while you keep the upper body erect go ahead and let the knees bend; squat down until your legs are as close to parallel with the floor as possible.

Begin to come back up but don't come all the way up. I'd like you to stop just at the point where your legs are almost locked out, but not quite. This will help keep stress on the quads and will really burn after a few reps.

Be sure to do nonstop reps and keep them high, let's say in the fifteen to twenty-five range.

Sissy Squat

The only thing—and I mean only thing—sissy about these is the name. Wait until you do a few reps of these and you'll see just what I mean.

I want you to make sure your feet and legs stay close together from start to finish. You'll probably need to hold onto something to help with balance, but only use it for balance and not to pull yourself up or take the work off of the quads.

Start by keeping your body straight; then bend at the knees and come forward while leaning back at an angle of about thirty to sixty degrees. Keep coming as far forward over your feet as possible until you can't comfortably go down any lower.

Keeping your body at this same angle, bring the body back up by extending the legs, but stop just before locking them out.

I want you to keep constant tension on the quads, and doing nonstop, nonlockout reps will really make them burn. The trick is to do high reps, as many as you can, and make sure you're resting no more than twenty-five to fifty seconds between sets and not resting at all between reps.

CHAPTER 22

THE HAMSTRINGS

Hamstrings can be a sort of forgotten muscle since they're not as visible as the front of the legs. However, for there to be balance—and you should always go for balance between body parts—you need to work the back legs equally as hard as the front legs.

Lucky for you, there are essentially two basic movements that will do a fabulous job in doing just that. Here are a few favorite hamstring (leg biceps) exercises that will do the trick.

Barbell/Dumbbell Stiff-Legged Deadlift

Here, you have your choice. With the barbell, you'll have a slight bend at the knees as, looking straight ahead, you bring your upper body forward over the feet and lower the barbell down to shin or foot level.

With dumbbells, you'll lower them down to the outside of your calves and not directly in front of your shins as with a barbell.

Excellent form is important for all exercises, but especially this one. I want you to focus on keeping your back slightly arched throughout the exercise, not allowing it to round over as you lower the weights.

Do reps in the seven to eleven range.

Standing/Lying Leg Curl

If you have a home gym multistation (such as a universal-type weight machine), you should be able to do leg curls either standing or lying or perhaps both. Regardless of which you choose, just be sure to follow a few pointers.

First, you want to isolate the hamstrings, and you do that by keeping the legs in a fixed position and only allowing the knees to bend.

You also want to curl the weight up or back as far as you can and try to let the ankle pads touch your glutes. If you're able to bring them up this far, you can be sure that your hamstrings are getting a good stretch and contraction.

I like to mix things up on this exercise. For example, one workout, you might want to do heavier weight and lower reps in the six to ten range. In another workout, try doing two or three sets of twenty-five reps. In another, just do one set of fifty to a hundred reps. Mix it up all the time. Just make sure you feel the leg biceps (hamstrings) squeeze, contract, and work hard.

LIFE LESSON

FOCUS YOUR ENERGIES ON THINGS IN THIRTY-, SIXTY-, AND NINETY-DAY INCREMENTS AND BEYOND

Our grand business in life is not to see what lies dimly at a distance, but to do what lies clearly at hand.
—Thomas Carlyle

One of the keys to being successful is to break down whatever goal you have into thirty-, sixty-, and ninety-day increments. Brief increments help sustain motivation, and because the time period is so brief, it's much easier for you to believe it can be accomplished and that results can be achieved.

Take changing your body. If you tell yourself that you want to lose thirty pounds by next year, that's too vague and unmotivating. However, tell yourself that you will lose three pounds in the next thirty days and not only is it doable, it's believable and highly motivating. And guess what? If you do the same thing for the next thirty days and the next thirty days after that, in twelve months you will have lost thirty-six pounds!

THE LESSON TO BE LEARNED

While you're doing a little something each day to help you reach your goal, stay focused on your long-term goals, but think future by taking the actions and adopting the behaviors and beliefs that support your better body/better life goal today.

THE CALVES

Hey, wouldn't you know that one of the best calf exercises you can do is one you can do at home, without any machines, and only needs the weight of your body and the help of a few stair steps! I told you working out at home would be easy.

I'm sure you've seen calf raises and the standing calf-raise machine at a gym. You know the one: your body is vertical, your toes are on a platform and you simply go up and down with only the ankles that bend as the heels come down and up as high and low as they can.

Essentially, you'll be doing the same exercise in just a slightly different way. You'll be standing on a stair step instead of a machine, and you'll be doing nonstop reps and lots of them, but for only one mega set.

Calves respond incredibly well to either heavy weight or high reps. High, as in fifty and more. In fact, to make it easy forget about counting reps; just count minutes. Start off by doing two nonstop minutes of calf raises all the way up and all the way down.

You're going to feel them burn like never before, and you'll want to stop when it happens, but don't. This is the point where you start making the exercise pay some big rewards.

When you can no longer do full-range reps, then do partial reps. Just keep the calves moving up and down until they can no longer do both.

I'm going to warn you right here and now: your calves will be sore for a good week or more if you do these the way I just told you. The rule I want you to remember is this: *Do not work the calves again until they have completely recovered from your last calf workout.*

If you can feel even the slightest soreness, even if it's been a good week or more, then take another few days longer before you work them again. This may mean that you'll only work calves three or four times a month and that's it. Oh, but wait until you see the results.

After a month or so of doing two nonstop minutes, increase the time to three minutes for the next month and then four minutes the following month after that.

Once you've increased the length of time, then start increasing the speed of your reps every once in a while for more intensity. Mix things up, try positioning your feet with toes pointed inward, or with toes pointed outward (ballerina style).

And always remember to stretch the calves by simply lowering your heels as far down as possible and holding them there for twenty to forty seconds after each calf workout.

CHAPTER 24

THE BACK

Basically, there are two types of back exercises: pulling and rowing. Even though both could be considered pulling, the pulling exercises I'm referring to are those such as pull-ups and lat machine pull-downs. For rowing, I'm referring to seated rows, barbell, or dumbbell rows. If your back workout has one of each type of exercise in it, you'll most likely be hitting most of the back.

Your back is a huge muscle group, and you'll get great results if you use exercises that will work it from different angles. For example, you might want to start off with seated low-pulley cable rows, then follow those with either barbell or dumbbell rows. Finally, if you still want to blast it,

try adding a set or two of chin-ups or machine lat pull-downs.

Form is a huge factor in getting the best from your back workouts. Try to avoid rounding your back when doing rowing exercises and do try to arch your back when doing pull-downs and rows.

Also, remember that the farther you can bring your elbows back behind you when pulling a weight into your body (like a row) or pulling a weight down toward your body (like doing a pull-down), the more you'll make the back muscles contract and the harder they'll work.

Here are some great back exercises you can do at home.

Chin-Up

I think this has still got to be one of the best back exercises around. Think about it: if you're able to pull your body up and down for reps, you're doing something. Don't get discouraged if you can only do one rep—just keep at it. Soon enough that one rep becomes two reps, then three reps, and so on.

Here are a few things to remember. First, the wider the grip, the more you'll feel it work the upper back, and the closer the grip, the more you'll feel it hit the lower back and arms. Many people think that the overhand-grip style of chin will tire their biceps out, but it's the triceps that are primarily worked when the grip is overhand. Switching to an underhand grip works the biceps.

Second: Allow the body to come up as far as possible and lower it until the arms are fully extended. You should feel those lats really stretching. Experiment with your grips: close grip, wide grip, overhand and underhand grips.

Third: Always make your first set your best set, since you'll probably have the most fuel and strength for one great set. Go for as many reps as you can on that first set.

Pull-Down (Using Various Types of Bars)

Same type of exercise as the chin-up, only you'll be seated and pulling the bar down to you instead of pulling yourself up to the bar. You'll like this exercise, since you'll be able to do so many different types of pull-downs simply by changing hand spacing and grip. Try pulling the bar down either in front or behind you and by using different types of bars and handles.

Stay firmly seated and arch the back, bringing the chest forward as the bar comes down to touch the chest area. Be sure to bring the elbows back behind your body to get that great back contraction.

Always let the bar come up all the way until the arms are fully extended so the lats will stretch.

You can do lower reps, but I think you'll find that higher reps of more than twelve will work great.

Seated Row

You'll want to be seated with the low cable about centered in the middle of your legs. A slight bend at the knees is okay. Grab the V-type handle or use an underhand grip on a straight bar and, with your upper body erect, pull the bar toward you until it touches your lower abdominal area.

As you pull the bar back, begin arching your back and your chest forward. As the bar comes back, focus on bringing the elbows and arms as far back behind you as possible.

As you begin to return the bar back to the starting position, allow your back to stay relatively erect, with only a very slight rounding forward in order to get a full lat stretch.

Reps in the eight to twelve range work well.

Barbell/Dumbbell Row with Overhand Grip

If you use heavy weights, this exercise will really put size on that back. There are different ways to do them. If using dumbbells, you'll want to have one leg (the leg on the side of your body that's not being worked) kneeling on a flat bench for support and the hand on that side holding onto the bench for additional support.

Bend the upper body at a near ninety-degree angle and, with the hand holding the dumbbell, allow the weight to come down below the bench until the lat is fully stretched. You'll then bring the arm and weight up until the weight is at your stomach level. Again, focus on bringing the arms back behind your body and keep the arm close to

your body throughout the exercise.

With the barbell row, using an overhand grip, you'll be using two arms instead of one (as in the dumbbell row) and you'll be standing with legs slightly bent and the upper body bent over at about a ninety-degree angle.

You'll take a grip slightly wider than shoulder-width on the barbell and then pull the weight up until it touches your stomach area. You'll keep the arms close to your body on the way up and really bring those elbows back behind you to contract those back muscles.

Do reps in the five to nine range.

Barbell Row with Underhand Grip

This will be the same exercise you just did for the barbell row, only you'll use an underhand grip instead of an overhand grip. Use a shoulder-width underhand grip and keep your legs slightly bent and your upper bent over at a forty-five- to seventy-five-degree angle.

Be sure to bring those elbows as far back behind you as possible as you pull the barbell into your lower stomach area.

Like the overhand barbell row, do reps in the five to nine range.

T-Bar Style Barbell Row

T-bar rows arc one of my all-time favorite back exercises, but most people who work out at home don't have a proper T-bar machine. The good news is this is not a problem! You can use one end of a barbell instead.

Load one side of the barbell with weights; the other side will be empty. Place the empty side in a corner so it won't move. Straddle the barbell so that the bar is between your legs. Your legs are slightly bent and your upper body is bending over so that your head is over the weights.

Wrap both hands around the bar near the top where the barbell sleeve joins the bar. Stretch those arms completely out, with your upper body in a locked position. Now, bring your arms up and your elbows up and back behind you until the weight touches your chest area. Slowly lower the bar back down and repeat.

Go for five to nine reps on these.

Behind-Back Trap Shrug

I'll have you finish your back workout with traps, but you should do them only once a week. Too much trap work can make your body appear too blocky.

Do this trap exercise with the barbell behind your back using a straight-up-and-down shrugging movement. With the barbell on the ground or on top of a bench, grab the barbell with an overhand grip.

Keep those arms fully extended and only move the traps and shoulders straight up and down. Think of bringing your shoulders up so high that they can almost touch your ears.

Do reps in the twelve to twenty range.

The Lat Stretch

Before and after a back workout, it's a great idea to stretch your latissimus dorsi, a.k.a. lats. Stretching helps keep your body limber and flexible, helps blood flow, and can help prevent stiffness and injury.

A great lat stretch also happens to be a very simple one. Take one hand and hold on to something vertical such as the supports on your weight machine or a doorjamb or anything that won't move.

Keep your arm fully extended and lean back. You should feel the lat on the side that you're holding (i.e., left arm, left lat) really stretch. As you're holding it, try moving your body around a bit. For example, allow your body to bend down and see how that feels. Then try moving your body away from your holding hand and see how that feels.

After about thirty seconds, switch hands and do the same thing for the other side. One of the other great things that stretching does is help create the mind-to-muscle link; thus, the next time you train, you'll begin to actually feel the exercise better and have more control in how you can direct the exercise to hit certain areas you're training.

CHAPTER 25

QUICK TIPS FOR BETTER RESULTS

Okay, time for some quick tips that will help take any exercise and make it an even better exercise.

I've always been a big believer that it's not about using a lot of weight as much as it is in feeling the exercise work. Making the muscle burn and pump. That's why I love using different angles, hand placements, and positions. I'll teach you some of them. Always use proper form and be thoroughly warmed up whenever using different exercises and forms. Slowly incorporate any new training method into your workout and be sure each matches your training experience and level of expertise.

Changing Your Grip

If you take a wide grip on a barbell and do a bench press, you will probably feel it in the outer pecs. However, bring the hands closer together and you'll feel it in the inner chest and triceps.

Remember what I told you about changing your grip from wide to close when you work your back? Using the same exercise, you'll feel it in different parts of the muscles you're working simply by changing handgrip and spacing.

Changing Your Grip (continued)

Changing the Angle

A great example I like to use is working the biceps. If you do curls standing up with the arms close to your body, you tend to feel it more in the upper biceps. However, squat down and rest the upper arms and elbows on top or against the inside of your legs and do a curl so that your arms are at more of an angle and you'll feel it more in the lower biceps.

Changing Foot Position

We're talking legs and calves here, and there are essentially three ways to change foot position to work the calf and thigh muscles in different ways.

For calves, if you point the feet straight, it tends to work the entire calf. Turning the feet outward will direct the work to the inner calves, and turning the feet inward will focus the work on the outer calves.

For legs, remember that feet positioned straight ahead will tend to more evenly hit the entire thigh area. Feet turned out will direct the work to the inner thighs and feet turned slightly inward will tend to shift the work to more of the outer thigh. To help prevent injury, on all leg work remember to keep the knee always in a line with the toes.

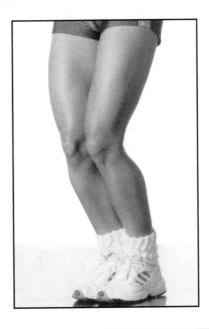

Changing Elbow Position

I know you probably wouldn't think so, but simply by moving the elbows up or down or into the body or away can affect how an exercise feels.

Let's take the dumbbell kickback. Most people will do this exercise with either their working upper arm close to their body or below their body. Wrong!

The trick is to keep the upper arm close to the body but make it come up above the upper body. Try this and you'll see. Do a dumbbell triceps kickback, and the higher you raise the working elbow and dumbbell above your body, the tougher this exercise will get.

You can do the same with the press-down simply by moving your elbows in close to your body or away from your body.

How about biceps? Like dumbbell curls? Good, you'll like them better by simply changing your elbow position. Do them wide, close, elbows forward, elbows back. You can do the same with barbell curls, cable curls, and the list just goes on. The most important thing to do is experiment and find your best elbow, foot, angle, and grip positions. They'll help turn good exercises into great ones.

LIFE LESSON

TAKE PERSONAL INVENTORY

It isn't lack of time that holds us back, it's lack of direction.

—Zig Ziglar

Take a look at your life, the things you've accomplished and the things you want to accomplish. Take a good look at where you are and where you want to be. You will be amazed to learn that one of the biggest reasons you haven't accomplished more, experienced more, or enjoyed more is because you've been a time waster. Workouts are no exception.

Has the majority of your free time been filled with activities that have been tension relieving or goal achieving? How many times have you heard the excuse that people just don't have time to do the things they want to do or say they will do?

The truth is lack of time usually means lack of direction. People have chosen to spend so much of their time majoring in minor things that they waste their precious time and their life.

Look at your life. Think back to how many precious minutes, hours, days, months, and years you have lost because you've wasted time. Whether it's getting the most from your workouts or anything else, you need to have a "vacation state of mind."

What's a vacation state of mind? Think about whenever you're getting ready for a vacation and you have an incredible amount of work and chores to accomplish in very little time.

Those days before a vacation, it seems like you'll never get all those things done. Ah, but what happens? You always seem to accomplish those seemingly impossible chores. Why? Because you become so incredibly focused that you give your mind a clear goal, target, and time limit to accomplish it.

THE LESSON TO BE LEARNED

Regardless of how busy you think you are, you will always find time to do the things that are important to you at that time in your life. While you may have lots of interests, you always find time to do the things you desire. Remember, interest and desire are two very different things.

Lack of focus in knowing exactly what it is you want to achieve is one of the greatest reasons why you waste time. The more you become locked in and believe that you can achieve any goal you set your mind to—a new way to look and feel, for example—you will all but eliminate the needless waste of the most precious resource you will ever have—time!

Tell yourself right now that you can and you want to use every minute of every day to the fullest. Make each day and workout count. Hold yourself up and expect more from yourself so that each night before bed you can look in the mirror and honestly be able to tell yourself that you've made the most of the precious time you've been given.

PEOPLE HAVE THE POWER TO
MAKE A DIFFERENCE IN THEIR LIVES.

—OPRAH WINFREY

Part V: The Mind

Mental Strategies and the Brain Principles

It's Finally Time for You to Meet Your Twenty-Four-Hour Servant

What if I told you that from the day you were born, you've had a hidden servant inside of you whose only job is to make sure your body stays healthy and your thoughts and beliefs come true?

And what if I told you that your hidden servant has worked for you—and only you—non-stop, twenty-four hours a day, every single day from the day you were born and will continue to work for you until the day you pass from this earthly plane? Would you believe it? You'd better.

Your unconscious mind has been that servant and tireless worker that has made you who and what you are—even given you the body you now have.

What Your Servant Wants You to Know

You see, your servant listens to everything you say and think, and it watches everything you do. Everything. Its job is never to question what you tell it, even if what you tell it is wrong. Your servant's job is to act upon your commands, and those commands are your words, thoughts, beliefs, mental pictures, and emotions.

If you've told yourself that you're fat and out of shape, that you have no energy, that you're tired, then you can be absolutely certain that your servant has heard those commands loud and clear. And its job is to make sure you stay fat and out of shape, have little or no energy and feel constantly tired, because that's what you've told it you wanted!

Remember, your servant doesn't question whether or not you truly want those things. Once you've told it the things you want or don't want, it makes no difference to your servant. Its job is to take your words—what you tell yourself and others—as its orders, and it will always make sure your orders are carried out. No questions asked.

The problem for the majority of people is that they keep their minds, words, thoughts, and beliefs focused on what they *don't* want instead of on what they *do* want. With such a powerful servant, is it any wonder that they keep getting more of the things they don't want and less of the things they do want?

Achieving a great-looking and great-feeling body is so simple, so easy, if you'll only learn to talk to your servant in ways that will make it help you rather than keep you frustrated.

It's time you learn how to do it.

How to Talk to Your Servant in the Language It Understands Best

What I'm about to tell you will radically and wonderfully change your body and your life more than I believe you may ever have imagined possible. I'm no miracle worker, nor will I ever claim to be. But what I'm about to share with you are things few people know and even fewer people use. But for those who do, and who use them the way you're about to, changes take place in their lives that seem spectacular.

Things You Must Never Tell Your Servant

Let's begin with the don'ts. Remember, you talk to your servant through your spoken and unspoken words to yourself or to others, your thoughts and your beliefs, your mental pictures and emotions. So . . .

- Don't tell your servant what you don't want to happen, such as "I don't want to be fat anymore" or "I always have trouble staying on diets" or "Nothing seems to work for me" or "I wish I didn't have to exercise so much to keep the weight off." Saying and thinking those things will only bring more of what you don't want into your life.

- Don't tell your servant that you're out of shape or want to lose weight, because what you're really telling it (your primary thought) is that you are fat, and its (your

servant's) job will then be to keep you right where you are—fat.

- Don't tell your servant that you've got a slow metabolism, because its job will be to do all the things it can to keep your metabolism slow, just like you've told it.

- Don't tell your servant that it's hard for you to eat healthy or regular nutritious meals, because its job will be to find ways, excuses, and beliefs that keep you from eating the things that are good for your body.

- Don't tell your servant that since you've had kids or gotten married or taken that new job that your body has permanently changed or you can't find any time to exercise. Because its job will be to reinforce all those things you tell it, by keeping you too busy and uninterested in exercise and eating right, thereby keeping you looking and feeling the same. You can't get mad at your servant, it's just doing exactly what you tell it!

I think you get the idea of what I'm saying. Keep your thoughts, words, beliefs, mental pictures, and emotions away from what you want to change, get rid of, or avoid. Think only of already having accomplished those things you want.

The Things Your Servant Needs from You

Your servant responds to words, mental pictures, and emotions much the way you respond to them. For example, how would you feel if someone told you, in a nice way, but without much feeling, something like "You look good"? You'd probably enjoy the compliment, but what if that same person told you, this time with lots of passion and emotion, "Wow, just look at your body. You really look incredible!" Big difference.

If you tell yourself with little or no emotion, with a fuzzy picture in your mind, that you look and feel pretty good, that does little to make big changes take place inside and outside of you.

Vividly picture your new body and tell your servant, with lots of powerful emotion, that you look and feel great and then watch what happens. Your servant goes into overdrive to make what you're telling it come true much, much faster.

The more descriptive and uplifting your words, the more crystal clear the mental picture of what you want, and the more emotion you put behind those words and pictures, the faster your servant will work to bring all those things into your life.

What to Say to Your Servant

Your servant wants you to tell it what you want as if you've already achieved those things in your life right now. That means if you weigh 160 pounds and want to weigh 130, you'd say something like this: "I look and feel fantastic at 130 pounds." What you're telling it is present tense, and what you want to happen is already happening right now and not at some future time.

I can hear you now, "So what you're telling me to do is to say something and believe it as though what I'm saying and believing has already happened, even though it hasn't?"

That's exactly what I'm saying and here's why. As you know by now, your servant listens to everything you think or say. If you keep telling yourself that you look and feel great at 130 pounds (even though you weigh 160), your servant must then make a choice; it has to either keep you at your same weight or override those old commands with the new commands you're now giving it.

If you keep telling yourself that you look and feel fantastic at 130 pounds and you do it at various times throughout the day (of course, more times than you keep telling yourself you're fat)

and with emotions you can really feel inside, then I ask you, which command do you think is going to win out?

You've got it: the new, more powerful one.

Nature doesn't like a vacuum; meaning, if you take away something, it wants you to replace it, or it will replace it for you. The same is true with your life, especially the thoughts you think. By replacing the old thoughts and beliefs with new, better, and more empowering ones, you're simply cooperating with the laws of Nature, and the result will be good for you.

Remember always to think of, talk about, and believe in whatever it is that you want in the present tense. Whatever it is you want, act as though you have it and are enjoying it right now, this moment and today!

Make your affirmations not only in the present tense, but make them positive and express them with lots of feeling. That's right—really feel what it would be like to have the body you've always wanted and to have more energy and look and feel like a million bucks.

I want you to think of the very best things that you could ever imagine and dream that could happen to you. Let that be the place where you begin and then build your life from there. Let that be the starting place for you. Just try it and get ready to be amazed at how different your body and soul will feel.

Be your own best friend and don't hold anything back when it comes to praising yourself, being good to yourself, and believing in yourself. And believe that whatever it is you want—and I don't care how silly or out of reach others have told you or you may have always believed it was— you can and you will have it!

Keep It a Secret

Don't tell anyone about your new way of thinking. No one. Right now, it's your little secret between you and your servant. Soon, and I mean very soon, people will notice big changes in you—from how you act to how you look and feel. All these things will be so noticeable that you'll have all kinds of people asking you to tell them your secret.

Don't be surprised when people come up to you and say something like, "I don't know what it is, but there's really something different about you." Just smile, because you know how it was then and how it is now. Yeah, Baby!

Over two thousand years ago, the great wise man Jesus summed up this whole thing beautifully. Pardon me as I paraphrase here, "Whatever you pray (that means whatever it is you're keeping your mind on, because your thoughts really are your prayers), believe that you have received it and you will have it."

Let me repeat that. Notice it didn't say that you could receive it or might have it. Believe that you have received—as in right now and not at some time in the future.

Talk to yourself in the present and your future will be just the way you want it. In the final chapter I'll give you some incredibly powerful thoughts and affirmations that will quickly help change the way you look and feel.

The 504-Hour Solution

The way you look and feel and what you have chosen to do or not do, eat and not eat, are the end result of your habits. Habits are those unseen, powerful forces that put your life on autopilot, so to speak.

Habits will either keep you right where you are or help you change your life to the way you want it to be. The choice is always yours, and habits simply follow the commands of your servant.

Think of it like this: What you think about and what you believe are the commands you give to your servant. Those commands that your servant

hears from you quickly become your new habits. Your servant faithfully follows your commands by developing habits that make the things you tell it come true for you.

Habits become like big steel cables, but they never start out that way. At first, as you begin taking new actions and forming new behaviors, the habits you are creating by doing those things are like thin string that could be broken at any time.

Yet, each day that passes and each time you do the same new actions and behaviors, that thin string becomes thicker and thicker and much harder to break, until after a very short time—for many people within thirty to sixty days—that thin, fragile string has become like a thick steel cable, incredibly hard to break.

Yes, all this happens so silently, so behind the scenes, and so quickly that before you realize you've got the habit, the habit has got you! That's one of the biggest reasons people don't look and feel their best, because they haven't learned what they must do to cut the old thick steel cable of bad habit and replace it with the brand-new thin string of the new and good habit they must have in order to achieve what they want.

I'm going to show you how to do it. It's called the *504-Hour Solution* and you will be amazed at how it will work for you. Five hundred four hours; do you know what that comes out to? Twenty-one days. Just three weeks and you can install a healthy habit in place of the old habit that may have kept you fat, out of shape, out of breath, lethargic, and frustrated by not looking and feeling your best.

Is it easy? You bet. Is it for real? Absolutely. Will it last? Oh, yeah. Will it work for you? There's no doubt about it. So how can you do it?

The 504-Hour Solution: Days One Through Seven

The first few days will feel a bit strange to you

because what you will be doing is giving your servant new commands and backing up those commands with action.

At first you'll have to consciously think about what you're doing; for example, starting to eat things that are good for you and cutting back a bit on fatty foods or doing a little exercise.

The benefit is that each day you do those things you are moving away from having to think about doing them to your brain doing them on autopilot. Imbed the blueprints into the unconscious, and give them over to your servant to remind you to carry them out.

I want you to think of creating a new habit in the same way that you learned a new task at your job. At first, you really had to think about it. Then, as each day passed, you became better and better at it until, very quickly, the task became so easy you could do it while you did many other things at the same time. What I'm teaching you here is essentially the same process, and it works incredibly well every single time.

All you have to do is *just a little bit* each day. I don't want you to push yourself and think you must do everything at once in order for it to work, because you don't. Start out very slowly and easily and each day just do a little bit more than you did the day before. That's all it takes.

The 504-Hour Solution:
Days Eight Through Fifteen

By about day eight, you should be feeling a little different inside. Instead of having to think so much about your new actions, attitudes, and behaviors, things should be getting much more instinctive.

You'll feel much of the pressure you've put on yourself—from wanting to do everything right and not forgetting anything—being lightened. It's at this point that you start getting glimpses, little previews of what's about to come in the next few days. That's a great feeling, which you're going to really love.

Again, don't push yourself too hard and only do a little bit at a time. Allow the changes to be easily accepted by your servant. At first, your servant will keep questioning if you're sure you want it to accept these changes. That's normal and will quickly pass. Remember, it's used to doing one thing and now you're telling it to do another.

Up until this point in your life, whenever you wanted to make a change and do something new, your servant did everything to resist those changes. And when you allowed yourself to be led by your servant into doing more than you should, because you were telling it to do something it was not commanded to do, its job was to reject anything that went against those old programs.

Why? Your faithful servant is only carrying out all those years of negative mental pictures, emotions, unwise thoughts, and beliefs you've told it you've wanted and accepted. Your servant likes things just the way they are because one of the main jobs your servant has is to keep your body and your life in balance—even if many aspects of your life are bringing you unhappiness.

Allow your servant to slowly, easily, and gradually accept those new, empowering, life-changing beliefs and actions and after a few weeks, watch what happens.

The 504-Hour Solution:
Days Sixteen Through Twenty-One

This is the time things start getting fun. By days sixteen through nineteen, you'll find yourself hardly having to think about your new actions and behaviors. Many people have told me it feels like they've handed the ball (the new actions, attitudes, beliefs, and behaviors) off to someone to carry for them. Well, wouldn't you know it, that "someone" is their servant, or unconscious mind, the true power source for any and all lasting changes you'll ever want to make in any area of your life.

The beauty of you holding back and not pushing yourself too hard or forcing those changes too fast is that as each day passes, you become stronger, more powerful, and more excited. For the first time in your life, you will have tapped into something amazingly powerful that's been locked up inside of you your whole life. A power that you never really knew existed or fully understood.

As each day passes, you will begin to see and feel what this awesome power can do for you. You will become excited to turn more of it on. By holding it back, it becomes, in a sense, like a racehorse for which you are holding the reins.

As each day passes and you get closer and closer to that twenty-first day, you start letting out a little bit more of the reins, thereby allowing your racehorse to sprint to the finish line—which, in this case, is made up of the positive new actions, attitudes, and beliefs that go along with the new body you want.

Once you reach day twenty-one, you can let go of the reins and allow your racehorse to gallop to the finish line the fastest way it knows how. The important thing is for you not to force your servant to go *your* own conscious way. Your servant knows exactly how it will get you there (in ways you may not presently consciously understand) and amazingly, it will do it in ways you probably never thought about.

Running Your Life on Autopilot for a Lifetime of Incredible Success, Experiences, and Rewards

Do you know what your racehorse—your unconscious servant—needs to keep running nonstop twenty-four hours a day? Just the affirmations, mental pictures, thoughts, and words that tell it you're happy and you're on the right course.

If you'll just be a little patient, enjoy the new habits you have created, do a little bit each day, and follow the guide I've just described to you, you will have the secret that will bring you all the changes you've ever wanted to make. Creating change will be easier and much faster than you ever imagined possible, guaranteed.

LIFE LESSON

THE BODY YOU HAVE IS THE BODY YOU WANT

Where the mind goes, the body follows.

Studies have proven an incredible fact: Your brain doesn't know the difference between a real or an imagined event. If you can vividly imagine doing something, yet you've never actually done it in real life, it doesn't make a difference to that brain of yours, because it will believe that you have.

Now take a good look at your body. What you see in the mirror is exactly the kind of body you believe you should have. After all, it fits perfectly with your mental picture of the body you think you should have.

That's a rude awakening for most people. After all, how can they be so dissatisfied with their bodies if that is the body they have always gone back to after diet programs failed and exercise programs got too boring?

THE LESSON TO BE LEARNED

It all goes back to those mental pictures you've been giving yourself. You see, your unconscious mind is that faithful servant I've been telling you about that never questions the commands or the mental pictures you give it. Its only job is to make the words you tell yourself and the mental pictures you give it come true, day in, day out, 365 days a year, and for the rest of your life.

If you want to look and feel different, you must first change the mental picture of how you look now to how you want to look, before you rush out to buy the latest infomercial gadget, get a personal trainer, buy new exercise clothes and videos, and start throwing out all those "unhealthy" foods for "healthy" foods. *You must first change the inside before you'll see any lasting changes on the outside.*

In the beginning, your mind will keep asking you and raising doubts as to whether this new picture is really something you honestly think you can achieve. That's perfectly normal, for, you see, the unconscious has always been trained to bring you that which is in perfect harmony with what you've always pictured and told yourself.

When some new picture or new commands and emotions are given to it, it first wants to reject them because they are different from what it's been used to. The key is to keep feeding your mind those new mental pictures of you *already* having and enjoying the body you want today.

That's right, act as if you already have it. The more you act as if it is already a reality, the quicker it will become a reality! Feel the emotions that go along with that new body. Feel the confidence and the energy. It won't be long before your subconscious mind will reject the old image of you, which will make the new image come true faster and in ways you've probably never imagined possible. I'll leave you with this thought from Dr. Joseph Murphy:

"What you think, you create; what you feel, you attract; what you imagine, you become."

THE MENTAL LAWS TO CHANGE YOUR BODY AND LIFE

Amidst all the mysteries by which we are surrounded, nothing is more certain than that we are in the presence of an Infinite and Eternal Energy from which all things proceed.

—Herbert Spencer

The Laws of the Body

What I'm about to tell you can radically change how you look and feel if you'll simply use them. I call them the *Laws of the Body*. People all over the world who achieve great success and who look and feel their absolute best use them, although they may not know the names of each of these laws.

Think of the Laws of the Body a bit like the laws in your city. The laws are meant to help you. When you follow them, you stay out of trouble; when you don't, then you've got problems. But the Laws of the Body go way beyond that.

The Laws of the Body never change. They will work for anyone, anywhere, anytime. The Laws of the Body will not work for one person better than another. They don't care if you're rich or poor, man or woman, young or old, in shape or out of shape. They are not influenced by a person's creed, color, ethnic background, or religion. These laws will work for you, whoever you are, if you use them the way they were meant to be used.

Let me repeat: The Laws of the Body will work exactly the same for everyone. The only difference between you and someone who gets incredible results is how well you use them.

The Laws of the Body are not visible or something you can read in a book or buy in a store. But make no mistake; the invisible is incredibly powerful. Think about it: the revolution and rotation of the earth, gravity, electricity, photosynthesis. All of these things are invisible, yet they use the laws of Nature and are totally predictable, unchanging, and awesomely powerful.

The Laws of the Body are the same as the laws of Nature, they work for anybody, anywhere, and at any time. I keep repeating that because I want you to get it into your head that the Laws of the Body will work incredibly well for *you* and not just for other people.

The universe operates by immutable, impersonal law: cause and effect. Our thoughts and beliefs determine what and how much we will experience in life. The life you have and how your body looks have been the result of your thoughts. *You change your thoughts, and you change your life.* Truly, these unseen thoughts are the most powerful force there is.

Even today, the majority of people don't know about these invisible laws, and many of those who do have chosen to ignore them; unfortunately, they do so at far too high a price. These are the same people whose lives are filled with worry, doubt, fear, superstition, negativity, money problems, health problems, and relationship problems. And what is left? Of course, bodies that don't look or feel their best.

Those who learn these new laws, who keep their mind fixed upon them and apply them in everything they do, will be bountifully rewarded. Soon you will be one of them.

Remember how I told you to use the 504-Hour Solution, by just doing a little at a time until your servant takes over? That's exactly how I want you to use the Laws of the Body. Start off slowly by using just one of the laws until your servant takes over and puts it on autopilot. When that happens, choose the next law and do the same. In a very short time, you'll be using all of the Laws of the Body—without even consciously realizing it—for results that will make you very happy.

If you're tired of struggling and beating your head against the wall for little or no reward, it's time to finally stop. It is time to learn the Laws of the Body. Remember to have fun, go slow, be easy on yourself, and use your servant.

The Invisible Law of Belief

Whatever you truly believe ultimately becomes your reality. You create whatever you experience in your life by your deep belief that that is exactly what you should experience in your life.

Right now, you look and feel the way you do because that's exactly the way you believe you should look and feel! You will only allow yourself to accept and experience those things for yourself that are equal with your belief.

Believe that you have no limits. Believe that you can do, be, and have anything you want. Believe that you can look and feel any way you want. You will achieve those things and more. Belief is the power that makes it happen.

The Invisible Law of Attraction

Your beliefs are a result of the thoughts you think. You attract to yourself, like the most powerful magnet imaginable, the people and conditions that match your thoughts and beliefs. Like attracts like, and you can't attract positive people and wonderful things in your life with negative thoughts and beliefs.

The key factor in determining how fast you attract the people and conditions you truly want—and how fast you'll change your body—is how much *emotion and desire* you give your thoughts and beliefs. The more emotion and desire you have, the faster that change will come to you. The less you have, the slower the change will happen.

The Invisible Law of Relation

Your outer world is simply a mirror of your inner world. If the majority of your inner thoughts are of wealth, success, and a great-looking body, then the experiences you have and the results you achieve will be those of wealth, success, and a new way of looking and feeling.

As within, so it is without, which means that the conditions of your life don't determine your thoughts; they were caused by your thoughts!

The majority of people think that changing their outer conditions—a new job, a new spouse, a new house, new clothes, a new gym, a new diet, or new area to move to—will change their inner life. But they are mistaken. Any change from the outside is only short term at best, very short term.

All lasting and permanent change for any and all things in your life must *first come from the inside,* and that means changing the thoughts and beliefs you have.

Thoughts and beliefs create reality, and you can change the things you are now experiencing and the way your body looks and feels by changing those thoughts and beliefs to be in perfect harmony with the new things you truly want.

The Invisible Law of Command

The more command you have over your life, the direction in which it is going, and the rewards and results you are achieving, the better you feel. The one thing you have complete and unchallengeable command and control over is your thoughts. For it is your thoughts and beliefs—which many think of as their faith—that create all the things you either experience or do not experience in your life. The choice has always been up to you.

The way to increase your command over every aspect and direction of your life is to take action to make your thoughts and beliefs come true. A great body doesn't just happen—you've got to work for it. You do that by using massive amounts of specifically focused, unrelenting action until you achieve your goals and dreams.

It's the only way you stay in the driver's seat and go to the destination you want and not where someone else wants you to go. Keeping your mind on what you want and off of what you don't want will keep you from feeling like a victim, which is what so many people believe themselves to be. Thinking your own positive and powerful thoughts gives you control over the events and circumstances of your life and your body.

No more will you be resigned to the idea, as so many people are, that you must accept the way you now look and feel, that you have to accept whatever bones or scraps that life may throw your way.

You are not simply a victim of circumstance, of whatever happens to you. You have, and always have had, the power to make your life and your body whatever you want it to be. You have always had the power to change the way you look and feel; all the power you will ever need is inside you right now, and there's no better time than right now to unleash it.

The Invisible Law of Expectancy

This Law of the Body says that you get what you truly expect, not what you say you want. You may ask, aren't both the same? Not at all.

For it is truly the things you believe you should have, yes, your deeply held beliefs about how you should feel and look, that determine what you'll allow yourself to have and experience in your life.

You may say that you want something different, but until your deep inner belief is changed, you'll keep getting the same things you've always gotten over and over. Same things with the same body—just a different day, a different month, a different year.

So how can you change your beliefs and use this law to get the very best so you can change how you look and feel? Glad you asked! Expectations are always equal to beliefs. Raise your beliefs and you automatically raise your expectations. Adopt the powerful life-changing belief that everyday, in every way, you are getting better and better.

The Body's Law of Substitution/Displacement

Nature loves when things stay the same. Whenever there is something missing, Nature fills what's missing right away so things can get back to normal. The same is true for the things you think about.

When it comes to how you look and feel, if all you've ever been able to focus on is how tough it is for you to diet and exercise, then as soon as you decide to get rid of those negative beliefs you create a vacuum. Nature doesn't want that to happen; it needs a filler.

You have to replace those old beliefs with new ones. Create new beliefs that will help you and not hold you back. When you do that, you're using the Body's Law of Substitution/Displacement.

This law says that if you're going to get rid of something, you must immediately replace it with something. Naturally, you want to replace it with something much better, something life-changing and empowering.

If you don't replace it with something you choose, then your servant will choose for you and find a belief that resembles what you are trying to get rid of. Yes, what you've been trying to get rid of. Remember your servant's job is to do what it has been trained and conditioned for. It will fight to carry out your original wishes, and those wishes come from the thoughts, mental pictures, and beliefs you have been thinking for so long.

When your servant does the choosing for you, the new belief it chooses will be much like the one you thought you finally got rid of. That is, unless you pick something positive to give your servant to use as a replacement for the old, painfully frustrating, wrong one.

When it comes to the way you look and feel, that positive something is the new beliefs (the right beliefs) that will end the failure cycle and replace it with a new cycle of constant, never-ending success.

I'm telling you as strongly as I possibly can that *never again do you have to be a failure. Never! From this day on, you will always be a great success. Don't you ever forget that!*

Replacing old beliefs is far easier than you

ever imagined possible. All you have to do is think about what you want to happen and to experience. Keep that mental picture burning in your mind with powerful feelings of having already achieved it, of already experiencing it.

Think about how wonderful you would look and feel having those things in your life right now. Think about why these new ideas and beliefs are the best for you now and in the future. Think about the joy and happiness you'll feel every day achieving those things.

Give your servant the reasons, with powerfully strong emotions, mental pictures, and desires, why you want these things in your life, how they will make you feel once you have them, and your servant will show you the best ways of achieving them.

The Invisible Law of Reaping and Sowing

Everything you have and are, everything you will ever be in your life is caused by something you either did or did not do. That experience, or lack of experience, is not caused by chance or an accident.

You may not experience the results of an action you took or chose not to take until much later down the road. But it always comes back to you, for as an unchangeable law, it must. Whatever you are reaping today is because of the beliefs that caused the actions you have sown in the past.

Think about it. If you want to have a fun and fulfilling life, you simply need to repeat the actions you took to cause those things. This same philosophy can be used to look and feel your best. Use the Laws of the Body, learn how to talk to your servant in the right way, eat right, exercise, get plenty of rest and relaxation; then, in a very short time, you will have a great-looking and -feeling body.

Likewise, if something is bringing you pain (like that out-of-shape body!), reflect on your beliefs, mental pictures, and actions that caused those things and retrain yourself to stop doing them. It will be amazing just how quickly the pain stops.

Sounds too easy, doesn't it? And that's why the majority of people don't believe it. That is why people continue to do the same old thing day in and day out, and, predictably, they keep getting the same painful results over and over again.

If your eating or exercise program made you fat and weak, would you keep doing it if your desire was to be firmer, stronger, and leaner? Of course not. You'd quickly change things.

And if your old mental pictures about yourself—how you look and feel—have been bringing you pain and frustration, why on earth would you keep torturing yourself by replaying them over and over? Simply change them to new pictures and watch what happens.

That's why it's so important for you change your thoughts and beliefs so you will choose to sow actions today that will only give you those experiences and things in your life that you truly desire tomorrow.

The Invisible Law of Increasing Returns

This means simply going the extra mile, doing more than what's expected of you. In life, you will always get more in return than what you give out.

For example, if you push yourself to do just one more repetition than you normally would on that tough exercise or eat one less scoop of ice cream, your body will reward you by getting a little firmer, a little stronger, and a little leaner. *Little actions produce BIG results and rewards.*

You'll find many other ways this law works in your life. Just keep in mind that if you go the extra mile in whatever you do, you'll receive rewards far in excess of any extra effort you've given out.

LIFE LESSON

BE HARD ON YOURSELF, BUT AT THE RIGHT TIME

*He who would do some great thing in this short life must apply himself
to work with such great concentration of his forces as, to idle spectators,
who live only to amuse themselves, looks like insanity.*

—Francis Parkman

Inside of you right now is a deep need to be pushed to your limits. This need, like many others, must be tempered, for too much of one thing leads to an imbalance in others.

Life is short, and for you to achieve any measure of greatness, you must listen to that inner desire to stretch yourself beyond the comfort level you've been so used to and to climb to a higher level of experience.

THE LESSON TO BE LEARNED

Pushing yourself to expand your possibilities and life experiences is a tremendous growing experience. And one of the best ways to prove that to yourself is by working out. You will be astonished at how your body will look and feel after only thirty days of hard training and healthy eating.

But working out is not the only way you can push yourself. Sometimes others can push us—positively, of course—beyond anything we've ever done. Sometimes friends will push you. Sometimes a spouse or the one with whom we're in a relationship will do it. However, many friends, spouses, or "significant others" don't fully understand what it means to push themselves, much less know how to do it for you. The real reward comes when you push yourself, for the winners in life do it consistently.

Don't wait for the perfect time or situation to push yourself. Each day the clock of your life is ticking. The time you waste right now is the time you won't have tomorrow to enjoy all the incredible rewards.

THE MAGIC POWER OF DISCIPLINE: HOW IT WILL QUICKLY AND EASILY CHANGE YOUR LIFE

Just one disciplined action will bring you many rewards.

Let me reveal another technique that will bring a tidal wave of changes in your life. How many times have you heard the word discipline? Many still think discipline is something you do to correct behavior. Many people think they've outgrown being disciplined, that discipline doesn't apply to them anymore.

Unfortunately, if you believe the same, you're missing the real meaning of discipline, because once applied, discipline can and will change any area of your life. To accomplish anything in life, the first step is taking action. If you never start, it's absolutely certain you won't arrive. Therefore, if action is the prerequisite to all success, then discipline is the engine that puts action into gear.

The more disciplined you are, the more you will accomplish and the faster you will accomplish it. Yet, being disciplined not only helps accomplish your goal; it can also bring you many other rewards just by sustaining that one disciplined action.

For example, let's say that you want to lose ten pounds of fat. So you take a disciplined action of doing just one thing, like eating healthier foods. Just look at what happens by you doing that one disciplined action.

- Your body has more energy because of the healthy foods you are eating.
- You feel better and not as sluggish.
- Your digestion has improved.
- You sleep better.
- Your complexion has improved.
- You're saving money because, on average, it costs you less to eat healthy foods than processed and junk foods.
- You're getting leaner each week—losing the fat and keeping your lean muscle tissue—because you're now eating foods containing the proper ratio of protein, carbohydrates, and fat.
- Now that you're feeling and looking better, your appearance is improving, thereby raising your self-confidence, self-image, and self-esteem.

- A healthy attitude will improve your relationships with others and your job performance, and it raises your belief in yourself that you can set goals and achieve them.

- Because you can see and feel the results from doing just one disciplined action, you now have a strong desire to try another, like beginning an exercise program. This will change your body and the way you feel even quicker.

Take a good look at that. *Ten benefits and rewards just by taking one disciplined action!* And you can experience the same number of rewards—and no doubt a lot more—by being disciplined in every area of your life. It seems that life has an unwritten code, and I believe it was Zig Ziglar who said it best, "The harder you are on yourself (the more disciplined you are), the easier life will be. Whereas the easier you are on yourself (the less disciplined you are), the harder life will be."

The choice has always been yours. Choose discipline and get ready for all the rewards.

CHAPTER

BRAIN SPEAK

Okay, so we've talked about your servant—or your unconscious mind—the 504-Hour Solution, the Laws of the Body, and discipline. So, I think it's becoming clear to you that the real answers to the question of how to look and feel great are never found in some magazine, infomercial gadget, or latest diet craze.

The real answers are, and will always be, found in your beliefs about how you should look and feel. Those beliefs will create the desire to do the things that will bring you the body you want.

I hope you're having fun learning this stuff, because it's making me smile right now as I write this. I've seen the changes you're about to experience in the faces and lives of people all over the world, and it always brings me incredible joy to know how great you're going to look and feel.

Right now, I'm going to tell you about how to use your servant for the most powerful ways to change your body and your life.

Five Unusual Ways to Use Each Success Experience to Redirect Your Brain for Greater Success

Whenever you give your servant too many beliefs too quickly, it tends to become overloaded and cause confusion. You need to prioritize your beliefs so your servant knows which one you want it to bring to you first.

Follow these guidelines to help your servant so it will not feel pressured and confused and will be able to help you in the best way.

One: Break Down Your Goal

Instead of telling your servant that you look and feel great at 125 pounds, when you weigh 150, simply tell it that you look and feel great at 147 pounds. A three-pound difference is very believable to your servant, and it gives it an easy goal to achieve.

Two: Reward Yourself

Simply tell yourself that setting and achieving goals is easy for you and that you're a goal believer and a goal achiever.

Three: Give It a Rest

Allow your servant to know that you are happy with how it is working for you by giving it a rest from achieving your weight-loss goal and having it work on a totally different goal for you. *Remember, your servant always wants a goal to work on.* Pick another goal that you'd like to achieve, such as becoming a more positive person. Take a few minutes each day to feed your servant a nutritious helping of positive thoughts and words found in books and tapes. Just a few minutes each day will pay *huge* rewards. After a few days of not making your servant work on fat loss, you'll begin to have feelings inside that your servant wants to go back to it again for you. It's a strange phenomenon. You tell it it's doing a great job and to stop working on fat loss, and it tells you that it doesn't want to stop and to give it more! But, it'll only do that when you don't force it and let it take you there at *its* own pace and not *yours* (that is, your conscious mind's).

Four: Re-evaluate the Goal

Now your servant is ready for a new fat-loss goal. This time give it the number 145 pounds. One to two pound increments are not only safe, they're believable and quickly achievable. After you reach 145 pounds, again give your servant a rest from fat loss before giving it a new goal. This time, pick a goal that's different from anything to do with fat loss or positive thinking. What about learning that new hobby you've always wanted to take up? Make your life exciting by always giving your servant new and fresh goals.

Five: Keep a Record

The next thing I want you to do is very important: Write down what you've achieved thus far and tape it up some place where you'll see it throughout the day. What this does is give your servant a constant thank-you for helping you to actually achieve those things and reminds you that you're on the right road to achieving more—much more. When your servant sees in writing, and not just in thoughts, mental pictures, and emotions, the evidence of what it has done and is doing for you, it's filled with more power to keep going, because it knows it's on the right track. For your servant and you, seeing the weight numbers drop from 150 to 147 to 145 and on down is a terrific boost and a reaffirmation that that weight number is doing nothing but going down—to just where you want it to be—and that you're a great success, which you truly are.

Final Thoughts

Remember, keep praising yourself and your servant for the great job you're both doing. Use the best words you can—the kind a best friend tells a best friend—and use written words and numbers so you can see in black and white just how great you're doing.

See, I told you it would be easy.

LIFE LESSON

THE CHANGE WILL DO YOU GOOD

We are not creatures of circumstance; we are creators of circumstance.
—Benjamin Disraeli

How many times have you heard that? Friends, coworkers, family reaffirming that whatever change you may be going through in your life right now will be good for you. Oh, but at the time, you don't want to hear that. The uneasiness, pain, and frustration you are feeling isn't comforted by words. The only thing that would help would be to be over it, and quickly.

The truth is, whether you are trying or not, you are changing every single day. The law of Nature says you either grow or die; there's no in-between. Most people resist change because they are so unsure of the outcome. They want to know all the answers up front, see every step that will be taken, and know the final result before they will act.

But life doesn't work that way; life works by unchangeable law, faith, and belief. You must have desire, belief, and faith for great things to happen in your life—like changing how you look and feel—then take focused action to ensure that they will.

THE LESSON TO BE LEARNED

Remember one of the great definitions of faith: "substance of things hoped for and the conviction of things not seen." What that says is you don't have to *physically* see what you want to have or to happen in order to have it or make it happen. You just have to have conviction and believe that it will happen and picture yourself already having it, right now, today. Forget about the exact steps you'll take to get there, because chances are, they'll be vastly different from how you'll actually reach it.

Look back at the kind of person you were twelve months ago. Reflect on how much you've changed, at how much your life has changed. You will soon realize that you are not the same person you were twelve months ago. Following that logic, you won't be the same person twelve months from now that you are today.

You're changing. Every day, you're evolving into a brand-new person, and that is exciting! The old you of yesterday is nothing like the new you of today and the even greater person you'll be tomorrow.

Embrace this change. Savor it, but most of all enjoy it! The best part of change is that you can be the one who decides how you will change. You can change into the kind of person you want to be. It doesn't matter what family, friends, or society thinks you should become. Change your body and your life so you are living the kind of life you dream of and truly want. Never ever accept anything less from yourself.

CHAPTER 30

THE PRINCIPLE OF POWER AFFIRMATION

WORDS YOUR BRAIN MUST HEAR TODAY FOR THE NEW BODY AND LIFE YOU WANT TOMORROW

You talk to yourself every day, and as you have learned, the things you tell yourself become the commands your servant acts upon to bring about those things in your life.

Affirmations are one of the most powerful ways to quickly and almost effortlessly change your life. You don't need to remember some complicated or long-drawn-out chant or mantra. Simply pick a few words or phrases that make you feel good and repeat them (with emotion) throughout the day.

You can either say them silently or out loud. Each will work great for you. People have told me they've gotten great results by saying their affirmations out loud in the car on the way to work, school, or wherever they were going. Others tell me they think about their affirmations silently in a place where they can relax, like a nice long, hot bath. Anywhere you choose is the right place for you.

I will give you one tip that makes these affirmations all the more powerful. Two of the very best times to say your affirmations are just before you go to bed and as soon as you awake in the morning. In the morning especially, your unconscious mind (your servant) is very receptive to what you tell it, since it hasn't had to deal with all the things your conscious mind gives it throughout the day.

Here are some amazingly powerful affirmations you can use to take you from where you are right now to anywhere you want to be. Remember, any affirmation you tell yourself must be in the present tense, as if whatever it is you desire to change is taking place right now.

For Overall Appearance and Weight Loss

- I look and feel great at _____ pounds.
- I'm full of dynamic energy, power, strength, vitality, flexibility, and endurance, and my body looks and feels like a million bucks!
- My servant guides me perfectly to perfect health and a great-looking body.

- Changing how I look and feel has never been easier or more fun.
- The body I have is the body I want, and I can quickly, easily, and permanently change it anytime I feel like it.
- People are amazed at how I transformed my body to look so great so quickly and easily.
- I am good to my body and my body is good to me.
- Getting myself in great shape is much easier, quicker, and more fun than I ever thought possible.
- I'm always the one who decides how little or how much and how quickly I want to change how I look and feel.
- I have the body, energy, and perfect health I've always wanted and I'm enjoying it right now and for the rest of my life!

For Energy

- I now have more energy than I've had in years.
- I always have plenty of energy to do all the things I want to do.

For Inner Power

- I expect the best and I get it every day, in every way in my life.
- Something incredibly great is happening to me today.
- My life and what I experience and how I look and feel has no limitations—none!
- My life is filled with perfect health, a fabulous-looking body, joy, peace, happiness, contentment, fulfillment, wisdom, knowledge, understanding, insight, wealth, success, opulence, riches, and abundance beyond my wildest dreams.
- I live each day to the fullest and I can't wait to see what life will bring me next.
- It's easy for me to separate the hype from the truth whenever I hear, watch, or read anything about nutrition, working out, and keeping my body looking and feeling its best.
- Every time I reach a goal, I reward myself in a special way because I am my own best friend.
- I love dreaming big dreams and setting big goals, because I'm a goal believer and a goal achiever.
- Life is a journey and not a destination, and I soak up each precious minute of each day and give thanks to my Creator for the gift of life I've been given.
- I laugh at all those silly infomercials and latest diet and fitness fads because I know and use the never-changing principles that have changed how I look and feel and my whole life.
- I freely share my success secrets with those who truly desire to change how they look and feel. I know the answers and feel really good inside anytime I can help others change their life.
- Working out has changed my life and I want to help others do it, too.
- The power to change my life is always inside of me. Only I have this power and only I can use it to change my life anytime I want.
- I think of the very best things that could happen to me and use that as the starting point for everything in my life.
- There's nothing that's too good for me.
- I am worthy and deserve to have, experience, and enjoy the very best that life has to offer anyone.

For Eating

- Eating healthy and nutritious foods is always easy for me.
- Healthy foods make my body look and feel great.
- I always choose the best foods for my body.
- I always know the right things to eat and I eat them.
- I always find the time to eat right and exercise, no matter how busy I am.

For Sleep

- I never have any problems getting a good night's rest.
- My body always gets the rest it needs.

For Stress

- My mind is at peace and nothing can upset me.

For the Past

- Everything I've ever done up to this day in my life has been a wonderful learning experience and has taught me lessons that will only help me in everything I do.

For the Negative Influence of Others

- I'm responsible for my own life and happiness. I love others but will not ever let what they say or think about me determine what I do with my life.
- I live by the belief that "What you or others think of me is none of my business."

- Other people will never know what truly makes me happy. I'm the only one who does and I give myself my heart's deepest desires freely and whenever I choose.
- I never compare my body or how I look and feel to anyone else. I am me. There is no one on this earth like me, nor will there ever be. That means I'm one of a kind and incredibly special, and I like that!

For Inner Guidance

- I listen to the silent power inside of me that perfectly guides me to the right thoughts, beliefs, foods, and exercises my body needs to look and feel its best.
- A strong mind creates a strong, healthy, and vibrant body, and my mind and body are the pictures of health, happiness, and never-ending energy.
- Life reveals its laws to me, and I use them to bring only the things that are in divine, perfect harmony and order for my life

For Exercise

- Working out makes me feel great!
- Day by day, my body is changing, and I'm loving it!
- My body always tells me how much exercise it needs, and I enjoy exercising it whenever it needs it.
- I only do the best exercises for my body and I'm incredibly rewarded in every way.
- I really enjoy giving my body just the right kind of exercise it needs to look and feel fantastic.

LIFE LESSON

YOU AND YOUR BODY

The way you look is not who you are.

For years I was the editor of the number one fitness publication in the world. I consider myself fortunate and blessed to have met many great people and to have learned from the greatest minds in health and fitness. There was one powerful lesson that I learned very quickly: Many people think of their body and who they are as one and the same.

Nothing could be further from the truth.

In traveling all over the world, I have seen how men and women have let food and exercise rule their lives to the exclusion of developing themselves mentally and spiritually. Is it any wonder they are still crying out for balance in their lives? For these people, their body image is their self-image. If they look good in the mirror that day, they feel good. If not, then their world is not a happy place to be.

What these people haven't realized is that how they look is based solely on their own perception, controlled by their thoughts and no one else's. Yet the inner turmoil and torment it can bring to them and to the lives of others is nothing to desire.

THE LESSON TO BE LEARNED

Your body was designed to do but one thing: carry your mind. More specifically, your brain. For, you see, your body can't think. It merely responds to the commands given to it from your conscious and unconscious mind. Remember your servant?

For you to look and feel the way you do now, you had to first give your servant a set of instructions (beliefs, feelings, and mental pictures) on what to do to make you feel and look a certain way.

From the types of foods you eat to how much sleep and exercise you get, your servant tells your body what to do and your body just responds.

Sure, looking healthy and being in shape helps you feel great and gives you more energy and power. But attaching more influence to it than to anything beyond that can cause you to look at yourself and life in ways that make you unhappy.

For example, your self-image and who you are as a person should never be dictated by how much muscle or fat you have, how lean or aerobically fit you are. These things are only the *effects* of your beliefs and actions and are not the *causes*.

Your body can look and feel any way you want it to. Sure, genetic predisposition may not allow you to have a different body type, but it will also not keep you from changing the body you have and making it as perfect as you want it to be within your genetic limits.

Really take the time to develop all areas of who you are. One of the most important things you can do for yourself and your happiness is to find balance in your life. You are equally physical, mental, and spiritual, with the spiritual being the most powerful and life-changing force of them all.

And finally, stay focused. Take action and keep taking action until you reach your goal, be it a great-looking and healthy body or anything else. If you can dream it, you can achieve it.

GLOSSARY

affirmations: Words and phrases that are repeated (verbally and/or nonverbally) to reinforce or change a condition or behavior. Affirmations work best when the word or phrase is stated in the present tense (e.g., "I look and feel great").

carbohydrates: One of the three macronutrients the body needs (along with protein and fat), found in many foods and used for energy and other processes.

cardiovascular system: Refers to the heart, lungs, and veins—the oxygen and blood transport system of the body.

complex carbohydrates: Foods such as vegetables, beans, grains, pasta, legumes, and brown rice.

fat loss: The process of losing excess fat stored in the body.

full range: Refers to the range of motion and type of rep used in training. Full-range training uses a wide range of motion.

glycogen: The fuel stored in muscle tissue that is used when performing muscular activity.

intensity: A method of increasing the effectiveness of exercise. Two weight training examples would be lifting heavier weights and decreasing rest time between each exercise, set, or rep.

lean tissue: Refers to body tissue primarily composed of muscle.

mental pictures: The mental images you create by imagining how a particular object, person, or experience would be.

metabolic boost: Anything that is used to increase the speed and/or efficiency of the body's ability to use nutrients.

metabolic rate: The "speedometer" that measures how quickly and effectively your body uses nutrients.

metabolism: The mechanism (brain and other organs) that directs how the body uses nutrients and other processes needed for living function.

partial reps: Refers to the range of motion and type of rep used in training. Partial rep training uses a limited range of motion.

push/pull: A training method that focuses on the specific action needed to work one muscle or muscle group using muscles that push away from the center of the body (e.g., triceps required to work chest and shoulders) to muscles that pull toward the center of the body (e.g., biceps required to curl for biceps or row for back).

protein: One of the three macronutrients the body needs (along with fat and carbohydrates), found in many foods and used for muscle tissue repair and other processes.

servant: Refers to the unconscious part of the mind that directs body functions where conscious control is not required, such as breathing, digestion, healing, memory, storehouse, and so on.

short range: A method of training that uses a small range of motion repetitions that concentrate on near-lockout movements (e.g., lowering the barbell only a few inches before returning to starting position as opposed to lowering it all the way down then pushing it back up again, as in full-range training).

simple sugars (carbohydrates): Such carbohydrates as fruits, juice, and honey.

skeletal system: Refers to the muscular system of the body.

weight loss: The process of losing excess pounds stored on the body. The loss of weight can come from water, lean tissue (muscle), and fat. Typically weight loss refers to the fastest and least permanent type of reduction.

zigzagging: Refers to alternating the amount of food you eat each day. For example, one day you consume 2,000 calories, the next day you consume 2,300 calories, and the third day you consume 1,700 calories, and so on for seven days. At the end of seven days, your total amount of calories consumed for the week remains the same, and the amount of calories you ate on any given day was the only variable that changed.

How You Can Contact Dr. Wolff

Over the years, people have asked if it is possible to contact me and if there are any other things I have written that may help them. The answer is yes! I'm happy to announce some exciting things that may be what you need. My official Web site is *www.RobertWolff.com*, where you'll find news on the latest books, tips, and motivational strategies that will help change your body and your life. And fitness-related information is only a small part of what you'll find.

The Lessons of Life

If I Only Knew Then What I Do Now: The Lessons of Life and What They're Trying to Teach You. This is the book I know will change your thinking and your life. In fact, I used a few of my Life Lessons and Mental Principles in this book, but there are over one hundred more you haven't seen that are amazingly powerful.

I believe one of the biggest reasons that people have enjoyed my writings has been because of the lessons I have learned in my travels all over the world. These are valuable lessons that I am happy to be able to share with you, lessons that will help you make a better life for yourself right now, and to achieve the things you want in your life.

My passion is positive power, motivation, and learning from life and from those who have gone through trials and struggles to reach their dreams.

These are people just like you and me, some famous, most not so famous, but all went through some incredibly tough times before they reached the good times.

The Lessons of Life encompasses the lessons of their lives, the lessons of my life, the lessons of your life, the lessons of all of our lives. This book was written for you, to inspire you and to show you that you, too, can reach your dreams, whatever they may be.

You will look forward to being inspired by this book every day. The lessons are quick and easy to read and you can choose whatever lesson best suits your needs for the day. A new day, a new lesson.

One of the reasons why everyone who has

read this book has enjoyed it so much is that you never have to read from beginning to end. Each day you can open any page in the book and find something that will touch your heart and soul for that day. I call it "The owners manual for life."

This is the first time this book has been available. Over the years, I've only given a few copies of it to close friends, who kept telling me to make it available to everyone because they enjoyed it so much and it inspired them and changed their lives. This book has the power to change your life, too.

And much, much more . . .

Visit *www.RobertWolff.com* often for the tips and inspiration you need to help you achieve the body and life you want. Here's to you, my friend, and to your great success!

Index

ABOUT THE AUTHOR

When it comes to fitness and motivation, Robert Wolff is in a class all his own. Dr. Wolff has worked with and interviewed the top names in fitness and health, including Arnold Schwarzenegger, two-time Nobel Prize winner Dr. Linus Pauling, sports great and boxing legend Evander Holyfield, and film stars such as Sharon Stone and many others. As former editor of *Muscle & Fitness* magazine and contributing editor to *Shape, Men's Fitness,* and many others, Robert Wolff's columns have appeared all over the world.